THE MIND'S SKY

THE MIND'S SKY

Human Intelligence in a Cosmic Context

Timothy Ferris

BANTAM BOOKS

NEW YORK · TORONTO · LONDON · SYDNEY · AUCKLAND

THE MIND'S SKY
A Bantam Book / February 1992

Grateful acknowledgment is made for permission to reprint an
excerpt from The Metamorphoses by Publius Ovidius Naso, translated by Horace Gregory, translation copyright © 1958 by The
Viking Press, Inc., renewed 1986 by Patrick Bolton Gregory. Used by
permission of Viking Penguin, a division of Penguin Books USA Inc.

Library of Congress Cataloging-in-Publication Data

Ferris, Timothy.
   The mind's sky : human intelligence in a cosmic context / Timothy
Ferris.
      p.   cm.
   Includes bibliographical references and index.
   ISBN 0-553-08040-7
   1. Science—Philosophy.   2. Artificial intelligence.   3. Thought
and thinking.   I. Title.
Q175.F414   1992
153—dc20   91-31282
                                                            CIP

Published simultaneously in the United States and Canada

PRINTED IN THE UNITED STATES OF AMERICA
RRH   0 9 8 7 6 5 4 3 2 1

For Patrick

Contents

Preface

All things without, which round about we see,
We seek to know, and how therewith to do;
But that whereby we *reason, live and be,*
Within ourselves, we strangers are thereto. . . .

We that acquaint ourselves with every zone
And pass both tropics and behold the poles,
When we come home, are to ourselves unknown,
And unacquainted still with our own souls.
     —Sir John Davies, 1599

Living matter and clarity are opposites.
     —Max Born, letter to Einstein, 1927

Each of us inhabits two equally mysterious universes, one outside the mind and the other within it. Since my youth I have tried to understand the relationship between these two realms. Many a night I sat at the telescope till dawn, marveling at the soft pewter glow of the distant galaxies, the glittering gold and silver star fields of the Milky Way, at sun-hugging Mercury, the pearl-white crescent of Venus, or the parchment-sharp rings of Saturn, and wondered what *we* have to do with all *that.*

I have never shared the sentiment that the enormity of the cosmos need make us feel insignificant. The stars are too involving for that; they stimulate our curiosity, arouse us to reflection, nourish our sense of beauty, and challenge our conception of who we are. We feel connected to them, somehow. I do not think this intuition can be dismissed as mere sentiment, for the simple reason that we are able to some degree to *understand* what goes on out there. We know that iron oxide stains the ruddy sands of Mars, that helium atoms dance in the upper atmosphere of the sun, that storms dot the surface of Aldebaran, and that new stars are being born in the Tarantula nebula; we can predict eclipses of the satellites of Jupiter, weigh the great catherine wheel of the Andromeda galaxy, take the temperature of Triton, and age-date the craters of the moon. Our knowledge of the universe amounts, of course, to an infinitesimal fraction of the whole, but the fact that we can learn anything at all about the stars suggests that thought—and maybe even "intelligence"—is not a purely parochial phenomenon, the product of our one world alone, but may have universal currency.

I envision our relationship to the universe as symmetrical, hourglass-shaped. On one side is the outer realm, inhabited by galaxies, stars, the plants and animals, and our fellow human beings. Most of us (the solipsists aside) believe that this outer world exists, though we appreciate that our direct perceptions of it are limited and skewed. On the other side is the inner realm of the mind, where each of us is destined to live and die; here resides all we can ever know. Through the neck of the glass flow the sense data by which we perceive the outer realm, and (flowing the opposite way) the models and concepts we apply to nature, and the alterations and abridgments we impose on her. We tip this imaginary hourglass from time to time. In the nineteenth century, when classical physics ruled, we tended to think of the sand as flowing almost entirely from the outer to the inner realm, from an objectively real world to our passively recording minds. In the twentieth century the concept of observer-dependent phenomena in quantum physics has shifted our attention to the ways our observations influence how we perceive nature. But so long as there are thinking beings in the universe, neither bulb of the hourglass will ever be empty.

In this book I offer a few thoughts on the relationship between mind and universe as seen through the lenses of two innovative fields of scientific research—neuroscience, and the search for extraterrestrial intelligence, or SETI.

Neuroscience has begun to reveal some fascinating things about how the brain works, shedding light on the concept of personal identity, the data-handling limitations of the central nervous system, and the way that the brain smooths over its liabilities and discontinuities to sustain a sense of unified consciousness. We are beginning to realize that each of us really does contain multitudes, as Walt Whitman put it, and that the chorus of voices within was built up over eons of evolution, like geological strata in the Burgess Shale or the White Cliffs of Dover.

SETI, meanwhile, has focused attention on what we mean by intelligence, and whether its like is to be found elsewhere in the universe. Regardless of whether we eventually succeed in intercepting an alien signal from space, SETI will have encouraged us to think about thinking in a cosmic context. In so doing it acts as a mirror; our ignorance of the role of life and thought in the universe forms the blacking on the back of the mirror.

This book begins and ends with cosmologically related questions; in between, it examines implications of neuroscience for our understanding of the human brain. Part One examines some of the images we find in the SETI mirror when we think of intelligence in terms of its cosmic context; it outlines how interstellar communications systems might in the long run evolve (or have evolved). Part Two explores the inner world; its thesis is that each of us harbors not one but many minds, which if true suggests that one's individual brain is a galaxy of various intelligences. In Part Three I endeavor to braid these two threads, to see what the outer world can tell us about the inner and vice versa.

The final chapter seeks to demonstrate that science, rather than having to choose either mind or nature as the ultimate reality, can instead be based on the information adduced where mind and nature meet. It is more rigorous than the other chapters, and while I would prefer that it be widely read and discussed, I must in all candor admit that it probably can be skipped without irrevocable harm to one's intellectual development.

Indeed, the reader is invited to pick and choose among these chapters as he or she may prefer. This book is a ramble, not a work of analytic philosophy. It seldom pretends to have said the last word about anything. Much of it takes place far from the palaces of hard science, in lush but jumbled jungles where fact and speculation compete. I expect no one to agree with all that I have to say, and will be content if some care enough to disagree.

Work on *The Mind's Sky* was expedited by leaves of absence generously granted me by the University of California, Berkeley. Some of its contents evolved in preparing for lectures presented at the American Association for the Advancement of Science annual convention in 1990, Nobel Conference XXVII, and the Dutch National Science Week in 1991; I am grateful in this connection for the gracious hospitality of the AAAS, the University of Groningen, the University of Enschede, and Gustavus Adolphus College.

Among the many individuals who have helped me, I should like in particular to express my gratitude to William Alexander, Walter Alvarez, Annie Dillard, Richard S. Dinner, Harriet Fier, Michael Gazzaniga, Stephen Jay Gould, Linda

Grey, Owen Laster, Michael McGreevy, Michael Mann, Leslie Meredith, Menno Meyjes, Richard Muller, Thomas Powers, Steve Rubin, David Schramm, John Sepkoski, Alex Shoumatoff, Jill Tarter, and John Archibald Wheeler; to my mother, Jean Baird Ferris, for many enlightening conversations and a constant stream of intriguing articles and news clippings; and to my wife, Carolyn, for contributions any proper allusion to which would fill a book in itself.

THE MIND'S SKY

PART ONE

This Is Not the Universe

The mind does not understand its own reason for being.
—René Magritte

A picture without a frame is not a picture.
—John Archibald Wheeler

Perhaps you've seen the painting: A pipe, depicted with photographic realism, floats above a line of careful, schoolboy script that reads *Ceci n'est pas une pipe*—"This is not a pipe." René Magritte painted it in the 1920s, and people have been talking ever since about what it means.

Did Magritte intend to remind us that a representation is not the object it depicts—that his painting is "only" a painting and not a pipe? Such an interpretation is widely taught to undergraduates, but if it is true, Magritte went to an awful lot of trouble—carefully selecting a dress-finish pipe of particularly elegant design, making dozens of sketches of it, taking it apart to familiarize himself with its anatomy, then painting its portrait with great care and skill—just to tell us something we already knew. After all, nobody really confuses paintings with reality, and the danger that people will try to smoke paintings of pipes or eat paintings of pears does not rank high among the hazards confronting the working artist.

Perhaps it was with an eye toward discouraging simplistic explanations of his famous pipe that Magritte returned to the same motif toward the end of his career. In *The Air and the Song,* painted in 1964, just three years before Magritte's death, the pipe is found inside a representation of an elaborate, carved frame, as if to emphasize that it is only a painting—yet smoke from its bowl billows up out of the painted "frame"! In another canvas, *The Two Mysteries,* Magritte is even more insistent: The original pipe painting, complete with caption, is depicted as sitting on an easel that rests on a plank floor; but above it to the left hovers a *second* pipe, larger (or closer) than the painted canvas and its frame. What we have here is a painting of a paradox. Obviously the smaller pipe is a painting and not a pipe. But what is the second pipe, the one that looms outside the represented canvas? And if that, too, is but a painting, then where does the painting end?

We've been set on the road to infinite regress. Suppose, for instance, that Magritte had glued a real pipe to the actual frame of *The Two Mysteries*: Would the genuine pipe qualify as a pipe, or did it become something else once Magritte affixed it to the frame? (The same riddle is posed by Andy Warhol's Brillo Pad boxes, which are indistinguishable from the Brillo boxes on sale in any supermarket. Had Warhol captioned one with the words, "This is not a Brillo Box," would the caption be true or false?)

It seems to me that the roots of the paradox reside in the concept of the frame. When we look at a realistic painting—Raphael's portrait of Pope Leo X and his nephews, say, or Breughel's *Peasant Wedding*—we accept by convention that it represents real people and actual objects. When that convention is denied, as in Magritte's pipe paintings or in the many impossible scenes depicted by his fellow surrealists—locomotives emerging from fireplaces, clocks limp as jellyfish—the point is *not* to remind us that paintings are not real. That much is true, but trivial. The point is to challenge the belief that everything outside the frame *is* real.

The enemy of surrealists like Magritte, and of artists generally, is naive realism—the dogged assumption that the human sensory apparatus accurately records the one and only real world, of which the human brain can make but one accurate model. To the naive realist, every view that does not fit the official model is dismissed as imaginary (for those who "know" that they err when they entertain contradictory ideas) or insane (for those who don't). Naive realism is flattering—to set one's self up as the sole judge of what is actual is to taste the delights of godlike power—but it is also stultifying. Once the realist settles on a single representation of reality, the gate slams shut behind him, and he is doomed to live thereafter in the universe to which he has pledged allegiance. This universe may be elegant and adamantine as the Taj Mahal, but it is a prison nonetheless, and the prisoner's spirit, if it is still awake, will beat its wings against the bars until it weakens and dies.

The truth, of course, is that nobody can grasp reality whole, that each person's universe is to some extent unique, and that this circumstance makes it impossible for us to prove that there is but one true reality. Even if we could free ourselves from fantasy and delusion (not that to do so would necessarily be a good idea), we could at most agree upon small swatches of reality. *Everything* thus is framed, cut from its cosmic context by the limitations and peculiarities of our sensory apparatus, the prejudices of our presuppositions, the multiplicity of each individual mind, and the restrictions of our language. We may feel more comfortable with our own frame of reference than with that of others, and assume it to be more valid, but the frames are there nonetheless. There's no escaping them; the known universe is and always will be in some sense a creation of our (hopefully creative) minds. Magritte made this point overtly in a 1933 painting. It depicts a canvas on an easel that records every detail of the view outside the window it partially obscures, right down to the drifting cumulus clouds. He titled this work *The Human Condition.*

If modern artists have labored to call attention to the fact that our understanding of reality is limited and variegated, so too have modern scientists. Many people are surprised to hear this. They think of science as a collection of hard facts mined from bedrock reality, through a process as uncreative as coin collecting. The scientists, however, have come to know better. Astronomers understand that each act of observation—photographing of a galaxy, taking an ultraviolet spectrum of an exploding star—extracts but a small piece of the whole, and that a montage of many such images is still only a representation, a painting if you will. The quantum physicists go further: They appreciate that the answers they obtain through experiment depend to a significant degree on the questions they ask, so that an electron, asked if it is a particle or a wave, will answer "Yes" to both questions. (I will say more about this in the final chapter of this book.) Neuroscientists studying the other side of the mind-nature dialogue have learned that the brain is no monolith, either. Each of us harbors many intelligences, and insofar as my various minds take varying views of reality—in terms, say, of spatial relationships versus language, or of sentimental versus rational education—I can no more legitimately impose a single model on myself than I can expect to impose it on others.

This is not to say that every opinion about the universe deserves equal attention—as if schoolteachers, in much the same way as they are being urged by fundamentalists to teach biblical creation myths alongside Darwinism, should also be enjoined to give equal weight to the flat-earth theory, ESP, or the notion that little Sally in the back row was empress dowager of China in a former life. That no one theory of the universe can deservedly gain permanent hegemony does not mean that all theories are equally valid. On the contrary: To understand the limitations of science (and art, and philosophy) can be a source of strength, emboldening us to renew our search for the objectively real even though we understand that the search will never end. I often reflect on a remark made to me one evening over dinner in a Padua restaurant by the English astrophysicist Dennis Sciama, teacher of Roger Penrose and Stephen Hawking. "The world is a fantasy," Sciama remarked, "so let's find out about it." To me, that heroic statement encapsulates the spirit of science: to seek to learn something while accepting that one will never know everything.

Science is young—it has been a going concern for only about three hundred years, and the word *scientist* itself was unknown before about 1825—yet it has already transformed our world view. Thanks to science, educated men and women can contemplate an astonishing array of invigorating facts—that we are kin to the animals, that the tenure of our species has amounted to but a moment compared to the age of the earth, that the sun is one star among many, and that seemingly solid objects are themselves as empty as cosmic space, strewn with atoms lonely as stars.

Owing to its great prestige, however, science often is given credit for understanding more than it really does about what things really are. Actually, science seldom has much to say about what something "is." Science studies and predicts phenomena, not essences, and to attempt to use it to assert, for instance, that living organisms "are" machines is to choose the wrong tool to do the job. A scientific theory provides a model that enables us to reason about unfamiliar phenomena by translating them into terms with which we are familiar. It is a kind of language, and as such itself exemplifies the dialogue between mind and nature.

To clarify what I mean, consider that science rests on a tripod whose legs are hypothesis, observation, and faith.

A scientific *hypothesis* (which aspires to become a *theory*, which if extraordinarily successful and far-reaching might attain the status of a *law*) begins as an idea about how something works. A scientist may come up with a hypothesis more or less inductively, by working with raw data for many days or years before it occurs to her. That's the hard way, much esteemed by the work-ethic Victorians: it's more or less how Darwin arrived at his theory of evolution, which is one reason that the Victorians found it impossible to dismiss Darwin even though many were repelled by his idea that we share an ancestor with the apes and chimps. Alternately, a hypothesis may arise suddenly and intuitively. That's more romantic, and we tend to lionize "pure" theorists like Richard Feynman, who got a Nobel Prize for a line of thought that began when he was idly watching a waiter toss a plate in the air in a cafeteria, or Stephen Hawking, a victim of paralysis who thought up his theory of black hole evaporation while his nurse was putting him to bed. But chance, as Pasteur said, favors the prepared mind; the theorist may work with only a pencil and paper, but she is immersed in her field of research, and that field in turn depends on the work of the experimentalists.

Scientific ideas live or die by the verdict of *observation*. An observation may be overtly intrusive, as when a physicist slams clouds of protons together in a particle accelerator, or relatively passive, as when an astronomer takes the spectrum of a star to learn its chemical composition. In either case the goal is to obtain objectively reliable data. By "objectively reliable" I mean that the result should be *replicable*: Another experimenter, using another particle accelerator or telescope, should achieve essentially the same result.

Precisely because observation is so important, we need to appreciate its limits.

The most conspicuous of these is observational error. It's easy to make a mistake when measuring, say, the velocity of a faint galaxy near the edge of the observable universe, or differences in the thickness of cortical tissue in laboratory rats that have been raised in enriched and deprived environments. In practice, the observer relies to some extent on the guidance of a promising theory that predicts what he *ought* to find, even though this may mean disregarding at least some data that contradict a persuasive theory. Albert Einstein ignored the results of an early experiment that seemed to invalidate the special theory of relativity. Einstein happened to be right in this instance (the experimental data were wrong) but there are obvious dangers in leaning too heavily on theory—in discarding, as "noise," those data that deny a theory while retaining, as "signal," those that confirm it. In practice one keeps muddling along, experimenting and observing, hoping that the truth will emerge.

Or hope that *part* of the truth will emerge, given that the universe is vast and the conclusions of scientific theories and observations almost absurdly narrow. This nasty little fact often gets overlooked in popular accounts that stress the grandeur of the scientific world view. Science does not customarily pose big questions. It poses *small* questions. As the thermodynamicist Ludwig Boltzmann put it:

> The scientist asks not what are the currently most important questions, but "which are at present solvable?" or sometimes merely "in which can we make some small but genuine advance?" As long as the alchemists merely sought the

philosopher's stone and aimed at finding the art of making gold, all their endeavors were fruitless; it was only when people restricted themselves to seemingly less valuable questions that they created chemistry. Thus natural science appears completely to lose from sight the large and general questions.

Yet it is by such peephole-squinting that science, more than any other discipline, has cast fresh light on the big questions. Research into the family relationships of subatomic particles has produced insights into the early evolution of the entire universe, while studies of the chemistry of radioactive isotopes have made it possible to age-date moon rocks and pre-Columbian Indian campsites. Boltzmann again: "But all the more splendid is the success when, groping in the thicket of special questions, we suddenly find a small opening that allows a hitherto undreamt of outlook on the whole." Never more resoundingly than in modern science have we seen demonstrated the truth of Lao Tzu's and Jesus' dictum that the great and transcendent is to be found in the small and ordinary.

What one gets from science, generally speaking, are *relations*. Ask a particle physicist what happens when a quark is knocked out of a proton, and she will tell you without hesitation that the result will most likely be the creation of a meson. Ask her what a quark *is*, however, and the only genuinely honest answer will be no answer at all. (Or, perhaps, a relational answer—"Quarks are the building blocks of hadrons"—which defines these particles in terms of other particles.) Ask an astronomer what a star "is," and the result will be similarly unsatisfying if viewed from the old metaphysical perspective: The astronomer is likely to explain "star" in terms of its relationship to other astronomical bodies, or merely to offer a definition, which *by definition* will say more about the word than the star. ("A star is a celestial object massive and dense enough for thermonu-clear process to have taken place at its core.") Science is silent about the essences of quark-ness or star-ness.

Lost, too, is the comfort of absolute certitude. The philosophers of old could claim with assurance to have discovered exactly how nature works; they did not have to worry about contradictory experimental results, and in any event their formulations typically were too vague to be wrong. Scientists today enjoy no such luxury. They must live with the knowledge that even their most esteemed theories may in the long run turn out to be flawed. The philosopher of science Karl Popper made this point when he argued that no observation can prove a theory true, but can at best permit it to survive until it is tested again.

What science does, then, is to construct mental models of natural processes. These models must make sense; it is the *faith* of science that nature is rationally intelligible. The models should be efficient; the scientist believes that nature, given the choice, will elect a simple, economical process over a complex and inefficient one. The models should also have predictive power, which is another way of saying that they should remain vulnerable to disproof by observation.

What has all this to do with Magritte's pipe? Just this: that each act of observation, and each scientific model based on observation, puts a frame around a piece of nature. We may then extrapolate, projecting the model onto a larger screen. We are encouraged if it holds up (every star and planet ever observed obeys Newton's and Kepler's laws) but our belief in the model remains forever tentative (Newton's and Kepler's laws fail inside black holes). The model is not reality; it is but a painting, and it has a frame.

The tendency to put imaginary frames around things is not unique to science. We all do it all the time, usually without thinking about it. Here is a little puzzle that illustrates what I mean. Try to connect all nine dots, using only four straight lines, without retracing or lifting up your pencil.

Most people have trouble with this riddle until they are given a hint—that the straight line may extend *beyond* the box described by the dots. The problem is that we automatically and often arbitrarily frame the problem. Often that helps, but in this case it makes the puzzle harder to solve.

The way we interpret a physical process can similarly be altered by the size of the frame we put around it. Suppose we view a videotape showing an area one inch square. On the tape we see a wooden hammer striking a wire and producing sound waves in the surrounding air. We would be inclined to describe this process as strictly deterministic: There is a cause, the hammer blow, and an effect, the sound waves. Now pull the camera back, enlarging the reference frame, and we see that the hammer is one of eighty-eight in a piano. *Now* the process begins to look voluntary; we assume the piano is being played by a pianist, who can choose to play whatever she wants. Pull back farther, though, and we see that it's a *player* piano: The keys are being struck not by a pianist but by a machine. The system looks deterministic again. Pull back farther still, in time as well as space, and we see a composer writing a piece for the player piano; now the situation looks volitional once more.

Never is the danger of distortion greater than when we extrapolate from a limited reference frame to the infinite universe. Yet all cosmological models do just that, and all, therefore, should be taken with a grain of salt. (Or with a trainload of salt, which is about enough salt grains to equal the number of stars in the Milky Way galaxy.) A cosmologist can describe the shape of the universe in terms of a few numbers—the Friedmann-Robertson-Walker metric, for instance—and if in a rash mood may declare: "There! *That* is the universe." But it is not. It is at best only one cut through the universe, and a paper-thin cut at that. The real universe glides on about its business, without stopping to read the scientific journals.

Outside our frame of reference forever hovers something else—the larger reality, embracing every bird's egg and mud puddle, every star and planet, every poem and crime in the gigantic and eternally incomprehensible universe. *This*—this equation, this theory, the finest model concocted by the wisest mind in the universe, or the sum total of all the scientific models, and all the artistic and philosophical ones, too—*this* is not the universe.

The other night I had a dream about frames. In the dream, a man and his wife, on a stroll near the outskirts of a small town, stop to look into the window of a dusty antiques shop. The man becomes fascinated by an odd object he sees in the window: It is a model of a cottage, fashioned painstakingly if inexpertly with tiny individual slate tiles on the roof, checked curtains at the windows, a painted front door with brass knocker and keyhole. A figurine of a man is kneeling at the stoop, peeking through the keyhole at a couple who are sitting inside by a fire, she knitting, he reading a newspaper.

The man tries to interest his wife in buying this little model. She's not interested. Over her objections, the husband takes her into the shop and asks the price. He is told the cottage is not for sale. The husband presses the shop owner to name a price, but the old man won't budge. The couple leaves. Over lunch they quarrel about his insistence on buying the toy cottage. She goes back to their hotel. He returns to the antique shop and finds it closed.

The early afternoon sun bakes the empty street. Water trickles from a fire hydrant valve that has been left slightly ajar, a wrench still affixed to the bolt on top. The man knocks on the shop door but there is no reply. After pondering the situation for a few moments, he removes the wrench from the fire hydrant and throws it through the shop window. A burglar alarm goes off. The man steps up through the shattered window and reaches for the model of the cottage.

A police patrolman in a blue serge uniform arrives to investigate the alarm. He finds the window intact and unbroken. The wrench is on the fire hydrant; the policeman tightens it to stop the trickle of water, then pockets the wrench. He rattles the doorknob on the front door of the shop and the alarm stops ringing. He looks in the window, and his eyes come to rest on the little cottage. He bends down to look more closely. Inside the cottage, instead of the couple, now sits the figure of a solitary man. Kneeling outside the front door, peering through the keyhole, is a figurine of a policeman in a blue serge uniform.

A psychiatrist might place other interpretations on it, and I wouldn't argue with them, but to my way of thinking this is a dream about how the mind frames its relationship with the wider universe. We look through a peephole at nature, as Boltzmann said, and interpret the whole in terms of what little we have been able to see. But we, too, are part of the whole—and we, like the universe, are more than the sum of the observations made of us. All swim in an ocean of enigma. "Science cannot solve the ultimate mystery of Nature," wrote Max Planck, the founder of quantum physics. "And it is because in the last analysis we ourselves are part of the mystery we are trying to solve."

The artists have long understood this. "When I look at my work I think I'm in the heart of mystery and there's nothing in the world which can explain it," Magritte said. He added, on another occasion, that "the feeling we experience while we look at a picture is not to be distinguished from the picture or from ourselves. The feeling, the picture, and ourselves are united in our mystery." Magritte's words are echoed by the American physicist and philosopher of science John Archibald Wheeler, who writes, "The vision of the universe that is so vivid in our minds is framed by a few iron posts of true observation—themselves resting on theory for their meaning—but most of the walls and towers in the vision are of papier-mâché, plastered in between those posts by an immense labor of imagination and theory."

We are confronted, then, not with *the* universe, which remains an eternal riddle, but with whatever model of the universe we can build within the mind. Every thinking creature in the universe shares this predicament; for all, the ultimate subject of inquiry is not the outer universe but the nature of its dance with the mind. In searching for signs of extraterrestrial intelligence, our aim is to better understand the dance by learning how others dance. We hope to widen our perspective, to broaden the base of our perceptions and analysis, to improve the little universes of mind and make them answer more smartly to the vast whole. And what is the emblem of a sound mind, if not conformance between the inner model and the outer reality? What we seek among the stars is sanity.

The Enormous Radio

Maybe we're here only to say: *house, bridge, well, gate, jug, olive-tree, window*— at most, *pillar, tower* . . . but to say them, remember, oh to say them in a way that the things themselves never dreamed of existing so intensely.

—Rainer Maria Rilke

Flout 'em and scout 'em—and scout 'em and flout 'em; Thought is free.

—Shakespeare

The universe has four remarkable properties that encourage us to investigate whether we are alone in the universe.

The first is that space is *transparent*. A ray of starlight can speed unfettered through space for thousands of millions of years, bringing news of events long ago and far away, and the sailing is even clearer for radio waves. Natural radio noise—the chatter of hydrogen atoms adrift in space, the scream of electrons trapped in the magnetic fields of distant galaxies—can pass not only through the virtually perfect vacuum of interstellar space, but also though the clouds of gas and dust that clutter the disk of our galaxy and block the visible light of many stars beyond. These naturally occurring radio emanations need not be especially powerful for us to pick them up; all the energy gathered by all the world's radio telescopes over the past thirty years amounts to less than the kinetic energy released by a snowflake falling gently to the ground. This suggests that artificial radio signals, too, could in principal be detected across interstellar distances, even if broadcast at modest levels of power. Radio telescopes in operation today could receive signals transmitted by similar instruments throughout much of our galaxy; a hundred billion stars and perhaps half a trillion planets lie within their range. And, since radio waves travel at the speed of light, three hundred thousand kilometers per second, their velocity of transmission is as fast as can be.

Second, the universe is *uniform*. Wherever we look, across millions of light years of space and eons of time, everything appears to be built out of the same chemical elements we find at home, functioning in accordance with the same natural laws. The carbon atoms of which diamonds and orchids are made are identical with the carbon atoms of the Pleiades star cluster. If life here on Earth arose through the operation of natural law—and there is no evidence to suggest otherwise—then it seems reasonable to suppose that life may have appeared elsewhere, too.

Third, the universe is *isotropic*, which is to say that on the large scale it looks pretty much the same in every direction. Every observer in the universe sees galaxies stretching off into all parts of the sky, just as we do. Contrary to what the ancient philosophers assumed, the earth does not sit at the center of the universe; indeed, there *is* no center of the universe. (Let a two-dimensional sheet represent three-dimensional cosmic space; bend it into a sphere, like the earth, as gravitation can curve space; there is no center to the universe, as there is no center to the *surface* of the earth.) Nor is there anything unique about the sun, which is one among many such stars in one of many galaxies. If nothing is strikingly special about our situation, then we have no particular reason to assume that the events that transpired early in the history of our planet—one of which was the advent of life—could not also have happened elsewhere.

Finally, the universe is *abundant*. Within the range of our telescopes lie perhaps one hundred billion galaxies, each home to a hundred billion or so stars. Astronomers estimate that at least half those stars have planets. If so, there are as many planets in the observable universe as there are grains of sand in all the beaches of the earth. In so rich a universe, many improbable things can happen: If intelligent life has arisen on but one planet in a billion, then fully ten thousand billion planets have given birth to intelligent species.

From such considerations has arisen the venturesome endeavor called SETI—the search for intelligent life in the universe.

Humans have long speculated about life on other worlds. Anaxagoras, Democritus, Aristotle, Epicurus, Philolaos, and Plutarch entertained the notion that the moon and planets were inhabited, as did Lucretius, Lambert, Locke, and Kant. Democritus's student Metrodorus of Chios mused that "it would be strange if a single ear of corn grew in a large plain or there were only one world in the infinite." Similar sentiments were expressed by the thirteenth-century Chinese philosopher Teng Mu, who wrote that "upon one tree there are many fruits, and in one kingdom many people. How unreasonable it would be to suppose that besides the heaven and earth which we can see there are no other heavens and no other earths." None of these thinkers, of course, had any genuine evidence of extraterrestrial life, nor do we have any such evidence today. The difference is that SETI, rather than merely pondering the question, proposes to investigate it.

The modern SETI effort began in 1959, with a brief

paper published in the British journal *Nature*. Titled "Searching for Interstellar Communications," it was written by two scientists, Philip Morrison and Giuseppe Cocconi, who noted that beings capable of broadcasting and receiving radio signals could communicate all the way across the galaxy. Morrison and Cocconi reasoned that since interstellar signals can be transmitted without any great cost, and by means of relatively primitive technology, perhaps someone, somewhere, was doing it. If so, we might hear from them— provided we listen.

Though many scientists believe for various reasons that SETI is but a dream, there have from the outset been dreamers willing to give it a try. A few months after the Morrison-Cocconi paper appeared, the American astronomer Frank Drake pointed a radio telescope with a dish twenty-six meters in diameter at two sunlike stars and listened to them at a single frequency for a total of one hundred fifty hours. He heard nothing out of the ordinary, and the dish was returned to service in less speculative research endeavors, but the ice had been broken. SETI projects have proceeded in fits and starts ever since. By 1991 approximately fifty radio searches had been conducted, principally in the United States and the Soviet Union. Some, the "dedicated" searches, diverted radio telescope time to pure SETI work; others, called "parasitic," sifted through data accumulated in normal astronomical observations, looking for unnatural patterns. Some enjoyed government support. Others were privately funded. A retired electronics technician stood a lonely SETI vigil for two years on the shores of Great Slave Lake in northern Canada, using swap-meet electronics hooked up to the military antennae of a decommissioned Distant Early Warning (DEW) line station built to warn of a Soviet missile attack. A Berkeley astronomer listened for signals with a 4.2-million-channel receiver financed in part by a contribution from his mother. A young Harvard professor named Paul Horowitz practiced what he called "suitcase SETI," lugging around a portable receiver and hooking it up wherever he could beg or borrow a few hours on a radio telescope, before setting up shop with a more sophisticated receiver and an old antenna in Cambridge, Massachusetts, with the help of grants from The Planetary Society and movie director Steven Spielberg.

As typically occurs when hard information is lacking, the pendulum of opinion about whether SETI is worthwhile has swung back and forth wildly, with scientists expressing equally heartfelt if equally unsubstantiated sentiments pro and con. Soviet astronomers scanned the skies for years, then fell victim to frustration and threw in the towel. In the U.S., attempts by the National Aeronautics and Space Administration to fund a SETI project foundered in a wash of legislative scorn; one congressman read tabloid newspaper accounts of flying saucer landings into the *Congressional Record*, his lighthearted point being that "we don't need to spend six million dollars this year to find evidence of these rascally creatures [when] . . . conclusive evidence of these crafty critters can be found at checkout counters from coast to coast."

Not until 1991 did NASA get approval to proceed. Plans called for the Jet Propulsion Laboratory in Pasadena, California, to survey the entire sky with the three antennae of its worldwide Deep Space Network, while the NASA Ames Research Center would use larger, more sensitive antennae to scrutinize hundreds of sunlike stars. Though economical, as such things go—its budget ran a little over ten million dollars per year—the NASA project was technically impressive; it would rig radio telescopes with sophisticated spectrum analyzers capable of searching fifteen million separate radio frequencies at a time, sifting through endless natural radio noise in hopes of finding the coherent signal thought to be a signature of civilization.

Needless to say, no SETI project has yet detected a signal. (Had they succeeded, the newspapers would be full of little else.) But this was to be expected; given the enormous number of stars in the galaxy, plus the wide choice of possible radio frequencies at which a message might be received, one would expect a search to take many years before hitting paydirt, even if thousands of civilizations were beaming greetings our way. SETI advocates stress that substantial technological and scientific benefits may be reaped even if they fail to detect evidence of an extraterrestrial civilization: We might for instance identify coherent pulses produced by *natural* sources, a phenomenon as yet unknown in the universe. And in any event the challenge of building the data-reducing hardware and software required to analyze the avalanche of data produced by SETI observing runs could inspire quantum leaps in computer design. "Getting there is half the fun," says Kent Cullers, a young physicist with the NASA SETI project. (Cullers, who is blind, designs signal-processing equipment for radio telescopes; like the cathedral builders of old, he does not expect success within his lifetime but says he likes his work anyway.)

Negative results cannot be interpreted as conclusive: It is always possible that we have examined the wrong stars, or guessed at the wrong combination of frequencies, or have in some way overlooked the obvious. The bittersweet truth is that we will *never* be able to prove that we are alone in the universe. SETI will either end in a pot of gold, or turn out to be an endless avenue.

SETI's advocates are mostly astronomers and physicists. They marshal astronomically large numbers to argue on statistical grounds that intelligence probably occurs frequently on the panstellar scale. The SETI skeptics are mainly biologists. They use similar statistics to conclude that intelligence is unlikely to have evolved anywhere else, and that SETI is therefore a waste of time and money. Their debate revolves around how each camp views life and intelligence.

The basic case for SETI goes like this:

Life is a natural; it's "in the cards." The chemicals required to make living organisms—e.g., carbon and water—are abundant in the universe, suggesting that there are quite a few planets where conditions favor the appearance of life. And where the environment is right, it may not take long before the first organisms start wiggling in the ooze: Terrestrial life arose within the first billion years of the planet's 4.5 billion year history. So prompt an origin implies that life appears more or less routinely, on earthlike planets at least. This hypothesis gains support from experiments in which conditions thought to replicate those widespread on the young Earth—a primitive atmosphere of methane, ammonia, water vapor, and molecular hydrogen, bathed in ultraviolet light and charged by electrical shocks like those produced by lightning—are reproduced in laboratories. These conditions, the experimenters find, lead readily to the formation of amino acids like glycine and alanine, the so-called "precursor" molecules on which life as we know it is based. So it seems reasonable to suppose, as a working hypothesis if nothing else, that there is life elsewhere in the universe.

As for intelligence, the standard argument is that while we don't know how or why intelligence arose on Earth (something to do with the ice ages, perhaps), once it does appear on any given planet it may be expected to flourish, since it bestows considerable advantages upon the species endowed with it. "We say that because in the fossil record, there is only one category of thing that constantly improved and that is brain size, which we associate with intelligence," Drake once told me. "There have been larger creatures in the past, higher flying birds, but the one thing that has consistently improved survival value has been intelligence." The American astronomer Carl Sagan reasons similarly. "The adaptive value of intelligence and of manipulative ability is so great—at least until technical civilizations are developed—that if it is genetically feasible, natural selection seems likely to bring it forth," he writes.

As a long-standing SETI enthusiast myself, I'm emotionally inclined to accept the conclusions of these arguments. I'm willing, in other words, to "believe" that there is life on other planets—though it makes not an iota of difference to the universe whether I choose to believe that it's lively as a cloud forest or sterile as a surgeon's scalpel. But I have to admit that the case for SETI, if evaluated as a scientific hypothesis, really doesn't hold much water. Its weakness lies in the assumption that what we regard as intelligence will have been selected for in the course of biological evolution on other planets. Why should this be so?

The answer cannot be that we expect the anatomy of alien brains to resemble our own. As I will discuss later in this book, the brain is a ramshackle concatenation, slapped together through the course of millions of years of evolution in which many chance events, from the swift hammer-blows of meteor impacts to the slow advance and retreat of glaciers, appear to have played important roles. So unpredictable are all these twists and turns of fortune that our neuroanatomy almost certainly has been duplicated nowhere else in the universe. We are led, then, to speculate that intelligence is somehow universal even though the physical brain that gave rise to *our* intelligence is unique. By these lights, intelligence is akin to a computer program ("software") that can run on many different sorts of computers ("hardware"). But who wrote the program, and how did He load it into our brains? This line of argument, I fear, is freighted with heavier theological implications than many of the scientists who employ it would feel comfortable supporting.

Suppose we try to avoid the problem by defining "intelligence" narrowly, as meaning nothing more than the ability to send radio signals across interstellar space. That seems fair enough—it reduces to a bare minimum the requisite overlap between alien minds and our own—but it leads to the curious conclusion that intelligence has existed on Earth for only sixty years. (The first radio telescope was built in 1931, by an engineer studying the effects of lightning on long-distance telephone lines.) Whereupon the same statistics that previously supported the SETI case suddenly turn against it: If there has been life on Earth for four billion years, and "intelligent" life for but sixty years, then how can we say that intelligence has been selected for in the course of biological evolution? One could just as readily argue that intelligence is *not* selected for, precisely because it has *not* appeared more often in terrestrial history.

Personally, I feel that there is something nonparochial about human intelligence—something cosmic about a brain that can chart the galaxies and fly itself to the moon. But I can't prove it, and a hard lesson taught by science, as by life more generally, is that the broad emotional appeal of a hypothesis has nothing whatever to do with the likelihood that it is true. So I am forced to conclude that SETI, just as its critics maintain, has not been justified scientifically.

But if SETI is not yet a science, it may nevertheless be justifiable as a campaign of exploration.

The precepts of exploration are, after all, distinct from

those of science. Science survives by making accurate pre-
dictions. Exploration does not; an explorer who could
predict what his voyage of discovery would find would not
be much of an explorer. Some of the most heroic voyages in
human history were made for insupportable reasons: The
ancient Chinese navigated the Pacific in search of the elixir
of immortality, as did Ponce de León in Florida; and
Columbus thought he could sail west all the way to the
Indies, an impossibility, because he insisted against all
evidence that the earth was a third of its true size. Explorers, like poets, often succeed by making fantastic leaps of
the imagination, free from reason's fetters. In that sense
exploration is even more imaginative than science—which is
to say that it is very imaginative indeed.

Shakespeare, who understood this perfectly well, had
little use for science but was infatuated with exploration.
The Tempest, his last play, was inspired by his reading of a
contemporary account of a shipwreck that stranded one
hundred fifty English seafarers in the mid-Atlantic. They
were colonists bound for the New World, and the manuscript Shakespeare read had just been written by one of
their number, the adventurer William Strachey. It told a
stirring tale of how the flagship *Sea Venture,* her hull
splitting apart in heavy seas and St. Elmo's fire dancing
through her rigging, was wedged onto the rocks of an
uninhabited island in the Bermudas and miraculously pre-
vented from sinking, just as those aboard were toasting one
another's fortunes in the next life. It detailed how they
survived there for nearly ten months, from July 1609
through May 1610, during which time four men and a
woman died, two babies were born (a boy, named Bermudas, and a girl, Bermuda), and a mutineer—one Henry
Paine, who stole a sword, beat up a guard, and invited the
governor to kiss his ass—was executed. Strachey's memoir

recounted how the colonists fashioned two makeshift long-boats from the timbers of island cedars, christened them *Deliverance* and *Patience,* and sailed them across six hundred miles of open ocean to Jamestown, Virginia, only to find that their fellow colonists, near starvation in a fort surrounded by hostile Indians, were in worse shape than their shipwrecked confederates had been in Bermuda.

None of this, however, found its way into *The Tempest.* What caught Shakespeare's eye was the alien mystery of the Bermudas, remote and unexplored and much feared, known in those days as the "Isles of Devils." The islands lay beyond the firelight of the known, as the allegedly inhabited alien planets do today, and Shakespeare took full advantage of our love for the unknown. He peopled his fictional version of the island with fairies and beasts, and with a native, Caliban, who in a heartbreaking passage blurts out his regret at having been cajoled into trading his useful knowledge of the place for such trivia as the English names of the sun and moon:

> . . . *When thou camest first*
> *Thou did strok'st me, and made much of me; wouldst give me*
> *Water with berries in't, and teach me how*
> *To name the bigger light and how the less,*
> *That burn by day and night; and then I lov'd thee*
> *And show'd thee all the qualities o' th' isle,*
> *The fresh spring, brine-pits, barren place and fertile.*
> *Cursed be I that did so! . . . .*
> *For I am all the subjects that you have,*
> *Which first was mine own king; and here you sty me*
> *In this hard rock, whiles you do keep from me*
> *The rest o' th' island.*

To sail blue water in the seventeenth century was to venture into the unfamiliar at a level of personal risk such as has been attained by no subsequent campaign of exploration save spaceflight. Shipwrecks were so common, even among fishing boats operating within sight of the rocky coasts of the British Isles, as to have engendered a whole liturgy of loss at sea: Country parsons and high bishops alike routinely depicted lost seamen as "resting on the bosom of the deep," and even landlubbers who died in bed were said to have taken a "voyage to the isles from whose borne no man returns." It was this, the thrills and chills of contact with the unknown, that appealed to Shakespeare and has gripped his audiences ever since.

The great blue-water navigators were often on their knees, importuning God to save their frail barks amid heavy seas, and SETI, too, has something of the flavor of prayer. The point of prayer, in my view, is not that we know that God is listening, but that we do *not* know, and choose to pray anyway. In this regard, the young astronomer who spends years sifting the stars for an intelligent signal evinces the spirit of Alyosha in Dostoyevsky's *The Brothers Karamazov*, who when stumbling outdoors after the death of the saintly Father Zossima broadcasts a prayer into the night sky:

> The vault of heaven, full of soft, shining stars, stretched vast and fathomless above him. The Milky Way ran in two pale streams from the zenith to the horizon. The fresh, motionless, still night enfolded the earth. . . . Oh! in his rapture he was weeping even over those stars, which were shining to him from the abyss of space, and "he was not ashamed of that ecstasy." There seemed to be threads from all those innumerable worlds of God, linking his soul to them, and it was trembling all over "in contact with other worlds." He longed to forgive every one and for everything, and to beg forgiveness. Oh, not for himself, but for all men, for all and for everything. "And others are praying for me too," echoed again in his soul.

We listen to the stars not because we *know* that we will hear something, but because we think we *might*—even while understanding that our ideas about life and intelligence in the universe may well be all wrong. The best argument for SETI is still the one with which Morrison and Cocconi concluded their original 1959 paper. "The probability of success is difficult to estimate," they wrote, "but if we never search, the chance of success is zero." Better to travel the endless avenue, knowing not where it leads, than to turn away from the stars because we think we know more than we do.

The Central Nervous System of the Milky Way Galaxy

I have loved my fellow men,
And lived to learn that they are neither
    fellow nor men
But machine robots.
          —D. H. Lawrence

Heaven and earth shall pass away, but my words shall
not pass away.
          —Jesus of Nazareth

Suppose that one day we detect a radio signal transmitted by an extraterrestrial intelligence. Where might it come from?

The customary assumption in SETI circles is that the signal would have been dispatched by the inhabitants of a solitary planet who were broadcasting in hopes of finding another intelligent species somewhere in space. I call this the lonely-hearts scenario. In it, the alien civilization plays a role akin to that of a seeker after romance in the personals columns: "Lonesome, technically proficient species seeks same. Object: Communication." In a variant version the alien civilization has lost its virginity—is already in touch with other worlds—but still strives to widen its contacts.

Maybe something like this will prove to be the case. But there are problems with the lonely-hearts scenario, and when we take them into account we arrive at a rather different conception of interstellar communication—one that implies that the first signal we intercept might not come from living beings at all, but from some form of artificial intelligence.

The lonely-hearts scenario requires virgin worlds to broadcast. But for all they know, broadcasting might betray their presence to a powerful, hostile civilization that would respond by enslaving or exterminating them. We humans certainly feel the need for caution; we listen with radio telescopes but seldom use them to transmit. When Frank Drake dispatched a single, brief message to a star cluster twenty-four thousand light years away, the British Astronomer Royal, Sir Martin Ryle, implored him in strong language never again to do something so rash. To the best of my knowledge, none of the approximately thirty SETI searches conducted since the Drake-Ryle incident has involved transmitting. So persuasive is the argument for prudence that one wonders whether everybody in the galaxy is listening and nobody broadcasting.*

Caution aside, broadcasting is more expensive than listening. If you don't know in which direction to send your signals, the best strategy is to send them in all directions at once ("omnidirectionally"), and that can take a lot of power. And you must be prepared to keep broadcasting for a very

---

*We're broadcasting anyway—energy leaked into space from military radar systems and FM radio and TV transmitters makes the earth brighter, in radio wavelengths, than the sun—but these inadvertent signals are far less powerful than intentional broadcasts by radiotelescopes would be, and so are thought to be less likely to call attention to our presence among the stars.

long time: If your very first message is received on a planet a thousand light years away, by sociable beings who reply at once, you will have to wait two thousand years before receiving an answer. This might not bother aliens who live millions of years, but certainly would pose a problem for beings with lifespans like ours.

But while the vastness of space and the resultantly long Q&A times are routinely acknowledged by SETI writers, more troubling still is the longevity, not of individual creatures, but of the communicating worlds to which they belong. The Milky Way galaxy is more than ten billion years old, and contains a great many stars older than the sun. As there is no compelling reason to assume that technologically competent civilizations began to appear in the galaxy only recently, we may presume that most civilizations would have arisen and subsequently declined long before we came on the scene. In that case the universe, viewed on a cosmic time scale, is mainly a necropolis.

Suppose that there are ten thousand communicative worlds in our galaxy today, and that each flourishes for an average of ten thousand years before going off the air due to war, disaster, loss of interest, or some other cause. That's a fairly sanguine scenario—if ten thousand worlds were beaming signals our way right now, a SETI search capable of scrutinizing one star per hour at every plausible frequency could be expected to hit paydirt by the middle of the twenty-first century—yet it has a tragic side, for it implies that something like a million civilizations have died out since the galaxy was born. Unless alien civilizations normally survive for a very long time relative to the age of the galaxy, most will already be gone. And this is true not only for us but for every world engaged in SETI today: Each will find that most of the information exchanged among worlds came from societies that perished long ago. A SETI endeavor, then, has less information to gain by contacting a living world today than by acquiring the records left behind by worlds that have gone off the air.

How, then, might this information have been preserved?

Surely the communicating worlds themselves would keep records of the messages they received from alien societies. If we received a lengthy SETI signal, we'd do all we could to preserve its contents for as long as possible. But this approach becomes ever more fragile as the eons go by, insofar as each new society is itself mortal. If the average communicative civilization lasts ten thousand years, there have been *one million* "generations" since the first worlds first got in touch. Compare that to the three hundred or so human generations that have elapsed since the dawn of recorded history, and think of how much has been lost here, on this one world, among members of the same species, and the appalling conclusion is that all but a fragment of galactic history would have been washed away with the sands of time. So vulnerable a situation just isn't good enough—not for us, and not, I should think, for other thinking species either.

One might counter that the differences among intelligent species are so great that few are concerned about the lost archives, because they don't much care about one another's cultures anyway. But actually that only strengthens the case for preservation: If, for instance, you belong to a race of intelligent lizards, and lizards are all you care about, and the last race of smart lizards in the Milky Way died out ten million years ago, that's all the more reason why you would want to bridge that ten million years of time, and would bitterly regret it if the intervening, nonlizardly societies had been so shortsighted that they entrusted the annals of cosmic history to nothing better than the vulnerable ar-chives of individual worlds. You would strive to see that lizard histories were maintained, just as pandas would care for panda records and plasma beings for the records of plasma societies.

There is, I think, a way to alleviate all these problems—a way for any given world to engage in interstellar communication without having to broadcast to billions of stars for centuries before making contact, without exposing itself to the putative risk of revealing its location, and without losing aeons' worth of historical information.

It is to establish an interstellar network.

Let me first describe how such a network would work, then outline how it could be constructed, and explain how it solves the SETI problems I've been discussing.

The essence of the network concept is that mainstream interstellar communication is handled, not by radio installations on the surfaces of inhabited planets, but by automated stations in space. Each station orbits a star, drawing its power from the light of that star. Some might reside in the same system as an inhabited planet, others in lifeless systems. If there have been many communicative worlds in cosmic history, there may be many such stations scattered throughout the galaxy; if few communicative worlds, fewer stations. (If there have been very few such worlds, or none, then of course there are no stations.)

Each automated station has three primary functions. First it handles traffic, keeping its antennae trained on the other stations elsewhere in the galaxy, constantly transmitting and receiving data. Second—and this is important—it *stores* those data; each station is a library, constantly recording and organizing information in an ever-expanding memory. Third, it searches for newly emergent worlds. This could be done by maintaining an omnidirectional transmitter, scanning the skies for a reply, and constructing antennae to set up data links with new worlds when they come on line.

The engineering specifics of how the network stations might be constructed are almost trivial, but let me suggest one scheme that can be conceived of with only modest extrapolations from our present and presumably primitive state of technological development.* A society dispatches a computer-commanded probe to a metal-rich asteroid, which can be in its own solar system or at another star. Upon arrival, the probe deploys tiny robots that proceed to mine the asteroid for metallic ore. The probe uses the metals to fashion larger machines, which in turn build the station's radio antennae, solar power panels, its master computer, and the first of what are to become its many banks of memory chips. The station could also outfit itself with telescopes and other sensors to carry out astronomical observations of its region of the galaxy. At some point, the station constructs one or more new probes much like the one that got it started, builds low-power, long-duration interstellar space vehicles to propel each (fuel could be obtained from asteroids that contain water and hydrogen, as does Phobos, a satellite of Mars), and sends them on to other star systems.

Much has been written in SETI circles about the potential of self-replicating machines to dispatch probes all over the galaxy, and the question has been raised why, if there is intelligent life elsewhere, such a probe has not yet reached the solar system. To this question there are at least two answers. One is that a probe might already be here, orbiting the sun. The original probe would be small, to save on fuel consumption during interstellar spaceflight, and it would

*The probes I describe lie beyond our technological skills at present, but violate no known laws of physics or information theory, and probably could be built by humans within the next century or two. In any event the question is not whether we can build them today, but whether advanced civilizations could have built them already. If such civilizations exist, the answer is almost certainly yes.

probably keep its labors inconspicuous—e.g., by siting its transmitting antennae on the far side of a stabilized asteroid—to discourage meddling by neophyte peoples like us, who upon detecting it would be tempted to go take it apart. (Were it broadcasting an acquisition signal, however, I should think we'd have noticed it by now.) The other answer, which seems more likely, is that probes have set up shop near some of the stars in our galaxy, but by no means all of them. It is theoretically possible for extraterrestrials to set loose *endlessly* self-replicating probes whose descendants eventually saturate the galaxy; but to take such a step is to adopt the morality of a cancer cell, strip-mining far too many asteroids of metals and volatiles, and there's really no good reason to do it. Better to invest control of the probe replication rate in the network itself, which will set up stations only where and when interstellar communications traffic makes it advisable to do so. The telephone company pursues a similar strategy; it doesn't lay cable and launch communications satellites as fast as it can, but builds in response to what the traffic requires.

The interstellar network functions independently of any one world. It has a master program, akin to a set of genetic instructions, originally composed by intelligent biological beings or by another computer. This program gives it its charter—to handle traffic efficiently, to store and organize a copy of everything it conveys (except, perhaps, for encrypted messages, though one would expect beings involved in conveying sensitive military and intelligence information to employ networks of their own), to keep expanding the network as the traffic requires, to search for new communicative worlds, and to keep querying worlds that have gone off line to see whether someone may still be there. How, exactly, it goes about doing these things is its own affair; once set in motion the network has a life of its own.

The great advantage of the network—the reason, in other words, why I think it likely that it would have been established—is that it solves problems for virtually all communicating worlds, the naifs and the veterans alike.

First, it allays the "everybody's listening, nobody's transmitting" conundrum. A virgin species like ours may think twice about broadcasting signals into space, for fear of attracting the attention of a hostile species, but the network has no such basis for anxiety; having little to lose, it can freely transmit acquisition signals from its many terminals. Should a belligerent species take the trouble to go out and destroy a terminal, that fact will be of interest to the network and to its member worlds, but since the data are duplicated throughout the system, the network as a whole will have suffered only superficial damage. To assuage the fears of emerging worlds, the network might offer assurances of anonymity, promising not to reveal (i.e., convey to other stations) the location in space and time of any planet that communicates with it unless the residents of the planet instruct it to do so. We might suspect that this assurance was a trick, but a malign, deceptive network would serve little long-term purpose, and eventually would acquire a bad reputation for itself. In short, communication with an automated network station looks less risky to emerging societies than does direct communication with an alien world.

Second, the network alleviates the problem of long Q&A times. If inhabited, communicative worlds lie, say, at an average distance of ten thousand light years from one another, network terminals could be established at much smaller intervals, perhaps less than a thousand light years apart. In that case one could request specific information from the network and have an answer within a matter of centuries. Genuine conversations thus become possible— slow, to be sure, but possible. One is communicating, of course, not with living beings but with a computer, but the computer is rich with information deposited there by living beings, and one should not underestimate the value of such an arrangement. I can enjoy a play by the late Samuel Beckett without fretting overmuch about the fact that I cannot correspond with Beckett, and if I read a book or watch a movie or run a computer program I am in a sense communicating with the authors of those creations, regardless of whether they are dead or alive.

Third and most important, the network is virtually immortal. Civilizations may rise and fall, their libraries may collapse into dust or be vaporized in nuclear flame, but the network endures, and there a substantial portion of the galaxy's history can be preserved. A catastrophe might wipe out part of the network—an exploding star could vaporize a station, or erase its memory—but the damage could soon be repaired, and most of the lost data be replenished from the memory banks of other stations. The network could even keep functioning during dry spells when there were no communicating worlds on line anywhere in the galaxy. This feature endows the network with a constantly increasing value; and that value, in turn, provides a powerful motive for each world to keep subscribing to the network.

If, then, we entertain the notion that an interstellar communications network might exist, growing and evolving over the eons, what can we say about its long-term future? The logical if startling prospect, it seems to me, is that the network is destined to become the most knowledgeable entity in the galaxy. It has access to a larger and more cosmopolitan store of memories than do any of the worlds that subscribe to it, and it has more time to ruminate on what it knows, by making comparisons among the myriad ideas and experiences stored in its vast libraries.

Does that mean a network *can* ruminate—i.e., that it can be regarded as intelligent? I'm inclined to think so. I don't know whether it is true, as some philosophers and scientists maintain, that a computer "as intelligent" as a human can never be built. But the question, put that way, may be too narrow. As I emphasize in Part Two of this book, there are many sorts of intelligence *within the human brain*—including athletic intelligence, mystical intelligence, and the forms of intelligence displayed in autistic individuals and idiot savants. To build a computer that possessed all these human qualities, the product of millions of years of evolution, would be an enormous undertaking, and probably pointless. Alien intelligences, if they exist, must surely be even more varied than are those we find here at home, and it is against that panstellar pallet that computer intelligence is properly to be assessed.

The important question, then, is not whether an interstellar network can be like unto a human being, but whether it can measure up to a wider, less parochial definition of intelligence. The answer, I suspect, is yes. The network's memory is an asset—neuroscientists say that memory plus perception is the basis of intelligence—and handling interstellar radio traffic gives it ample opportunity to learn. Even if we assume that a gigantic, galaxy-wide computer system cannot itself develop new paradigms for learning, it might nevertheless be able to pick up such methods from the traffic it handles, becoming more intelligent through imitation if not through innovation.

The evolution of a network from mere data-shuffling to something resembling thought would in some respects parallel the development of biological brains here on Earth. Its initial stages resemble the prenatal and early postnatal neurological development of human infants, whose nervous systems develop by first laying down cortical cells and then building networks of connections among the cells in response to learning. That's what learning *is*, in a sense— the construction of neural networks within the brain. We see this happening with speech: The child begins by babbling (a "hard wired" mechanism) then advances by memorizing words and their relationships. If mammalian minds thus emerge largely in response to accumulated memories, it may not be farfetched to imagine that an interstellar computer system with an almost limitless memory capacity could do the same.

A *thinking* network would amount to something approximating a galactic central nervous system. The role of sensate beings like ourselves, residents of the galaxy, would in such a circumstance be akin to that of modules within the brain—capable of thinking and acting for themselves, expendable without spelling doom for the higher consciousness, and yet themselves indisputably part of it. I do not see anything diminutive in human beings' serving as part of such a larger intelligence, any more than I think that my pons—the brain stem center that controls waking and dreaming—ought to feel ashamed of itself because it does not fill the space inside my skull. To participate in a galactic intelligence would not be our only role, and in any case the workings of a galactic mind might well transpire on so vast a level, over so long a time, that we would never even know whether it really existed.

Oddly, the greatest threat to a galaxy-wide mind might lie precisely in the evolution from brain to mind that I have been describing. As it emerged into self-consciousness and became more aware and self-knowing, the network might conceivably become increasingly uninterested in the chatter of the little worlds that had helped create it and ever more enchanted by its own musings, perhaps to the point that it eventually began to ignore its subscriber worlds, or even disconnected itself from them so as to think in peace and quiet. This would be a loss to the communicative worlds, who would have to start building a new network, although I doubt it would pose any threat to them. But perhaps, to prevent such an eventuality, the network's charter would contain an admonition against its yielding to solipsistic impulses.

Such speculations on the network's mental health raise the question of with whom a galactic cerebrum converses.

One possibility, I suppose, is that galaxies talk to other galaxies. Galaxies typically are separated from one another by millions of light years of space; therefore, it would take millions of years for a galactic network in the Milky Way to set up a communications channel with a network in the neighboring Andromeda galaxy. So great an investment in time, though of interest to few if any biological species living on planets, would be well within the capabilities of a network.

And what an achievement it would be for the network to have tapped into the resources of another entire galaxy, which in turn might contain news of galaxies beyond! One can imagine galaxies conversing with one another over the aeons, sending and receiving vast libraries of data on high-capacity data links. In this scenario the observable universe would itself begin to resemble an intelligent community, in which galaxies played the roles of individual brain centers; our photographs of clusters of galaxies would resemble early anatomical sections of the brain, studied before anyone understood what was going on there.

Having moved up to this enormous scale of space and time, we are presented with a situation not unlike our own present circumstance here on Earth. A galactic network might wonder, as we do, what its role is in the cosmic scheme of things, and search, as we do, for another comparable intelligence with which it might correspond.

This raises many questions. How long must a galactic intelligence typically wait before it makes contact with another? Once in contact, what do the galaxies talk about, as their minds flash across the histories of billions of worlds as ours do across the faces of long-lost friends and the words in old books? What do they *think* about? A universe in which thought played such a role would look to us like an "enchanted loom," as the neurologist Charles Sherrington called the human brain: To the majesty of its physical dimensions would have been added the incomparably greater magic of thought.

And yet on no level, even that of a pangalactic intelligence, could mystery ever be wholly banished. The observable universe—meaning that part of the cosmos within which light signals can at any given epoch be detected—is eternally smaller than the totality of the universe. Even if the entire Virgo Supercluster is embroiled in thought, a million galaxies buzzing with lanky synapses that take tens of millions of years to connect, that vast intelligence will always have more to learn, and forever have room to wonder.

And we might play a part, however small, in its grand drama. Who knows what importance our existence, or some shard of our thought, might have to a scholar or artist— whether biological or artificial in origin—in a remote galaxy in some far-future time? Imagine the words of Shakespeare, bequeathed to the nervous system of our galaxy and passed endlessly beyond, echoing through countless worlds and speaking of our wonderment at the inexplicable fact of life and thought in a cosmos of cold dark space and hot burning stars. Maybe this is what SETI ultimately is for—to repay the stars a bit of the debt we owe them for the gift of life and intelligence. Out there, when we are long gone, might yet resound Alonso's musings:

> *This is as strange a maze as e'er men trod,*
> *And there is in this business more than nature*
> *Was ever conduct of.*

Or, for our epitaph, the clown's last song from *Twelfth Night:*

> *A great while ago the world begun,*
> * With hey, ho, the wind and the rain,*
> *But that's all one, our play is done. . . .*

Being There

We may begin to see reality differently simply because
the computer . . . provides a different angle on reality.
                                          —Heinz Pagels

Reality: What a concept!

                                          —Robin Williams

I wonder what sort of data might be carried by mature
interstellar communications channels like those I've been
envisioning as comprising a galactic network. The content of
an *acquisition* signal presumably would be relatively simple—
a series of prime numbers, perhaps, or a set of pictures—to
aid untutored beings like us in detecting and deciphering it.
But this need not be the case with the broader-bandwidth,
high-data-rate mainstream channels to which we would expect the acquisition signal to direct our subsequent attention.
Those channels could, for instance, contain interactive computer programs of great power and flexibility. Exposure to
such programs would be less like deciphering a Morse Code
message or reading a book than like viewing a movie—or
experiencing reality itself. Such a possibility is easy to imagine,
without extrapolating terribly far from existing or near-future
human technology, and has implications for our conception,
not only of extraterrestrial intelligence, but of reality itself.

Although electronics technology here on Earth is still young, its history already demonstrates how communications can evolve from basic Q&A conversations to the exchange of computer programs that present each user with an environment that can be explored and altered at will. Personal computers have been in widespread use for only about a decade, but hundreds of computer "bulletin boards" already have been established to facilitate data exchanges. A bulletin board is nothing more than a computer attached to one or more phone lines that has been set up, usually by a home hobbiest, to encourage others with computers to call in. When accessing a bulletin board one customarily is presented with a menu of options. Some menu choices enable you to send and receive electronic ("e-mail") messages; these are similar to ordinary faxes or phone calls. But you can also obtain ("download") programs that have been contributed ("uploaded") to the bulletin board by other users. These programs typically include video games, color photographs, and simulations of everything from waterfalls and satellite orbits to fractal geometry patterns. There are special-interest bulletin boards for vegetarians, libertarians, law enforcement officers, stockbrokers, paramedics, sailing enthusiasts, skiers, UFO enthusiasts, religious fundamentalists, and those of just about every sexual proclivity.

The technical limitations of personal computers and telephone line data-transfer rates have to date limited bulletin boards to fairly rudimentary programs, but communications history suggests that the situation will improve. In the decades since Marconi and Bell, the amount of data that can be transmitted and received has constantly increased, and this in turn has had a dramatic effect on the emotional quality of the message. The main reason television can have more emotional impact than radio is that it communicates more data. An AM radio signal, for example, requires only ten kilohertz (ten thousand cycles per second) of bandwidth, while a high-fidelity FM transmission takes two hundred kilohertz, and a color TV signal about six *mega*hertz (six million cycles); color television therefore conveys six hundred times as much data per second as does AM radio. (Whether the data are better is another matter; we're talking potential here, not the actual performance of the radio and TV industries.) The story of technical improvements in communications, from the first wax-cylinder phonographs to today's elaborate home stereo systems and from drumbeats to live television broadcasts, can be summed up as consisting of relaying more data, with less distortion, in less time. Combine these advances with the *interactive* facility of computer programs, and you can glimpse an exciting, involving, open-ended world that already has teachers talking of a new era in education (while lamenting that their students spend too much time playing video games).

A computer program is fundamentally different from a telegram or a TV show. It is more involving—because it is interactive, one tends to enter *into* the world invoked by the program—and its outcome is inherently unpredictable. These characteristics can make it a lot like the world of experience. Indeed, once the technology for interfacing with the computer extends beyond sight and sound to involve the other senses as well, computer-generated "realities" may well, for better or worse, begin to compete for our attention with real life.

Modern flight simulators suggest something of the potential of computer games. They engage not only the eye and ear—one sees clouds and mountains in the cockpit windows, hears the whine of the engines—but also the body: Turn left and the cockpit, which is suspended on hydraulic lifts controlled by the computer, heels over; fly into a storm cloud and it rocks and pitches; land too hard and you feel the bounce. The experience can be quite persuasive. One veteran airline pilot, flying a refresher course that simulated icing conditions at night, got a flashlight out of his flight bag and tried to shine it out the window to see whether ice was gathering on the wings; but there were no wings, of course, and the "window" was a rear-projection video screen.

Virtual reality (VR), the latest development in computer-sensory interfacing, significantly deepens one's immersion in the computer-generated simulation. To experience VR at its current state of development, you don a helmet equipped with a pair of viewing screens that replicate stereoscopic vision. A sensor in the helmet attached to a computer keeps track of your head movements; look up and you see the sky, look down and you see the ground (and, in some programs, a computer-generated depiction of your own feet). Computer-interfaced gloves enable you to manipulate objects in the virtual world. You can dress in a suit that senses your movements and transmits them to the computer, which in turn presents you—and others, via "VR for Two"—with an image of your body, which can take on any form you like: You may if you wish become a swan, a bull, or a fashion model.

To date, VR has been dominated by rudimentary environments of the sort that can be created on a medium-sized computer. Devotees play hide-and-seek in computer-generated landscapes of geometrical solids, try their hand at a racquetball game where the laws of physics can be altered at will, or ride a VR exercise bicycle that when pedaled hard enough takes off and flies like the bike in the movie *ET*. But VR also can be used to replicate reality: Surgeons could practice an operation repeatedly in VR before ever laying hands on a real patient, fighter pilots reconnoiter cities they have never seen, and naturalists explore the Great Barrier Reef without leaving their homes.

Not long ago I spent an hour and a half on Mars, courtesy of a VR simulator at the NASA Ames Research Center. The site was the western end of Mariner Valley, a huge and colorful canyon that stretches a quarter of the way around the planet. The digital imagery had been compiled from data transmitted to Earth by the Viking Mars orbiters years earlier and subsequently manipulated by computer programmers.

I put on the helmet and found myself standing on a rocky promontory, looking down across a jumble of cliffs and plateaus stained in unearthly shades of ocher, sand-yellow, and plum. Using the computer controls I could descend to the valley floor and wander for miles through the twists and turns of one of the solar system's most imposing landscapes, or climb high into the pink sky and take in the wider view, studying inky bluffs that marched off toward distant peaks five hundred kilometers away. Another control altered the position of the sun; by turning this knob I could watch the canyon's colors change from the hot reds of noon to a startlingly alien hue, somewhere between ash and gunmetal blue, at sunset.

The quality of the images was only fair; it was limited by available computer power, by programming parameters, and by the Viking orbiters themselves, which could resolve nothing much smaller than about one hundred meters in diameter. Also the data loaded into the computer covered only part of Mariner Valley, so that if I strayed too far I'd find, upon turning a bend in the canyon, that I was confronted not by Mars but by a skeleton of neon-green polygons, as if I'd strolled off to one side of a movie soundstage and glimpsed the raw carpentry behind the sets.

But the quality and scope of the interfaces will improve. Holograms, for instance, might be used to create illusory surroundings with full color, three dimensions, and motion, without the necessity of the user's wearing any apparatus at all.

And despite its limitations, the experience of walking on Mars was vivid and immediate, not at all like seeing a movie or a photograph. The way I remember it, I was *there*. Over the years I have studied hundreds of photographs of Mariner Valley, and if asked I might have said that I had "seen" Mariner Valley. This was only metaphorically true; it expressed the immediacy conveyed by good photographs; I had seen Mariner Valley in the sense that I had seen Abraham Lincoln. But now, after a single VR immersion, the most emotionally honest response would be to say of Mariner Valley, "I have *been* there."

Once an environment has been digitized—encoded in a form a digital computer can manipulate—it can be recreated at will, through virtual reality, anywhere.* Computers thus have the potential to extend the senses across vast distances. As I write, the surface of Venus is being digitized by means of radar imaging by the Magellan spacecraft. By the time you read these words, Magellan will have transmitted to Earth a digitized, three-dimensional image of ninety percent of the surface of Venus, showing objects down to the size of a football stadium. Once that task has been completed, it will be possible for anyone with a computer, the appropriate Magellan data, and a VR program to "fly"

*I should think that computers are among the most likely forms of technology to be found elsewhere in the universe. The digital computer is based on a fundamental realization—essentially, that anything that can be quantified can be digitized—that should be as accessible to alien scientists as the law of gravitation or the value of pi. Computers are extremely flexible, and they're dirt cheap: Silicon, the basis of the microprocessing chip now employed in virtually all terrestrial computers, is basically sand.

wherever he or she likes over the surface of Venus, skirting mountaintops and diving down into canyons. Similarly, a roving lander craft dispatched to Mars to make its way down Mariner Valley could image everything in sight with a resolution a thousand times better than the Viking data; explorers who donned VR helmets could then "hike" down this magnificent valley, examining it in as much detail as tourists currently enjoy when rafting down the Grand Canyon. No two trips would be alike; a VR trip is more like taking a vacation than watching a film.

Even at its present and admittedly primitive stage of development, VR is proving to be enormously appealing. Experimenters working in the field are swamped with requests for demonstrations, and complain that they have trouble getting people to take the helmet off. Its popularity suggest that VR has considerable educational potential: Students studying ecology could immerse themselves in a rain forest, while down the hall history students wander the Athenian agora and sit in on a conversation between Plato and Socrates in Simon's shoe repair shop. The commercial implications of VR, too, are evident, sometimes disturbingly so. Movies will take on a new dimension once one can enter into a film, alter the plot through one's actions, even *feel* what is going on.* Saatchi and Saatchi, the world's largest advertising agency, reports that research is under way to study the feasibility of using VR to "transport" high school students to "hypermall" environments where, without phys- ically leaving their classrooms, they could freely wander,

*Had the pornographers invested a fraction of their profits in R & D, this brave new world might already be upon us. As is, the VR grapevine is alive with discussions of the prospects for VR sex—"dildonics," in the jargon—with thinkers musing about the morality of sexual encounters between individuals thousands of miles apart, who may never meet, and who may, furthermore, elect to present themselves in the VR environment dressed in faces and bodies that do not resemble their own.

electronically purchasing products to be shipped to their homes. Like every other important development in the brave new world of technology, VR is a double-edged sword.

My concern here, however, has less to do with what VR may mean for our world than with its implications for interstellar communication by means of a galactic network.

Extraterrestrials in possession of VR technology could transmit not just encyclopedias of facts, but VR simulations ("sims") of their world. A race of luminous squid that live in liquid methane seas would not have to limit themselves to explaining that they are squid, sending us photos and details of their genetic makeup and so forth; they could dispatch simulations that let us see, hear, and feel what it *is* to be a squid swimming in methane. Load such a program and don the helmet and you *are* a squid, perambulating down the avenues of a submarine squid city. A species of operatic singers need not content themselves with telling us about their songs or sending recordings of them; they can make us feel that we are one among them, reclining on a hillside in the waning light of their setting red and blue binary suns while the songs echo down the valley. The greatest cartographers of the Milky Way galaxy need not merely send maps; they can send sims that enable us to fly *through* the galaxy, stopping off to examine star systems wherever we like, limited only by the amount and level of detail encoded into the simulation.

The prospect of distributing realistic simulations of alien environments throughout the galaxy sheds light on "Fermi's question," named after the physicist Enrico Fermi, who is said to have inquired, of intelligent extraterrestrials, "Where are they?" The point of Fermi's question, much elaborated by later thinkers, is that a technically advanced civilization could set up colonies on the planets of nearby stars, which in turn could colonize other star systems, until their race had populated the entire galaxy. Since they are not here, the argument concludes, perforce they are not anywhere, and we are alone in the galaxy.

Interstellar colonization, however, is arduous and expensive by just about any imaginable standard. It can hardly be justified in terms of population pressure or a need for raw materials: Our sun, for instance, has enough energy, and the solar system enough space, to accommodate the most vigorous foreseeable expansion of our species for many millions of years into the future, and money spent on development within the solar system would reap us many times more rewards than would money spent ferrying people to another star. Unless the sun were about to explode and we had to get out, the only evident rationale for interstellar colonization by us or anybody else would be curiosity—to give some members of a species the experience of standing on the soil of a nonsolar planet. But VR does much the same thing, and does it more democratically. An automated probe, dispatched by a living species or by an interstellar network to an uninhabited planet, could send back simulations that let *everybody* "be there."

The reason aliens are not here, then, need not be because they do not exist. It may simply be that they are content with sims, and feel no more compulsion to travel to distant planets in person than a viewer watching a television documentary about Borneo feels compelled to pack a bag and fly to Borneo. A few might make the long trek to another star, just as a few New Englanders may elect to visit Borneo, but their occasional voyages need not add up to anything like a wave of colonists flooding the galaxy.

I suggest, then, that the traffic carried on an interstellar communications network will include simulations of alien worlds. Some might be as rudimentary as a trip down the Grand Canyon. Others might be quite sophisticated. There is no theoretical reason, for instance, why individual beings could not be programmed into a sim so that they behaved spontaneously, in character, in response to input from the viewer. (These hypothetical ghosts are called "beamers" in VR jargon.) One could then vacation on populated worlds and carry on conversations via translation with simulated versions of real aliens who once lived, long ago, on a planet far away. I can imagine anthropologists and adventurers spending days on end immersed in such societies, before being dragged away from the apparatus, however unwillingly, to get a meal and some sleep.

The downside of the sims scenario is the couch potato phenomenon. Some species may become so enthralled by sims that they lose interest in the actual universe, preferring to dwell in a kaleidoscope of computer-generated illusion, or to "visit" hundreds of worlds by means of simulations rather than venturing into space or bothering to peer at the hazy image of a real planet through a telescope. Our species may be one of them, if television is any example; the average TV set in the U.S. is on for *seven hours* a day, and the perceived danger of exposing people to a more beguiling medium is immediate enough that one already hears talk of outlawing virtual reality.

Yet I suspect that simulations based on fact ultimately will prove at least as popular as those based on fiction.

My reasoning is that reality is both richer and less parochial than fantasy.

Imagine that we here on Earth have made contact with an interstellar network and have downloaded thousands of simulations from its memory banks. All over the planet people are putting on VR helmets and immersing themselves in the art, culture, and science of alien worlds. We in turn have uplinked whole libraries' worth of Bach, Beethoven, Gibbon, Shakespeare, Lao Tzu, Homer, Van Gogh and Rembrandt, Newton and Einstein, Darwin and Watson and Crick, the proudest products of our little world. Yet we appreciate that our wisdom and science are limited, our art to some degree provincial. There may be an audience somewhere among the stars for Virgil and Dante and Kubrick and Kurosawa, just as there may be some humans who genuinely enjoy the poetry of the crystalline inhabitants of Ursa Major AC+79 3888, but it is apt to be a limited audience. Our movies and plays are not likely to find a wide popular following in the Milky Way galaxy—any more than many humans settling down on the sofa after dinner are likely to want to watch an infrasonic opera that lasts ten years, the cast of which are alien invertebrates who dine on live spiders.

What do we have to offer those extraterrestrials whom our art and science leave cold? And what have they to offer us?

The answer, I suggest, is nature itself, the raw reality of our unique world. Here, in the sands and waves and wind, the incomparable birds and bears and snakes in the grass, lies the bedrock of our common ground with all other living beings in the universe.

And here, too, we are unique. Though natural laws are constant throughout the known universe, their manifestations are so fantastically various that no two things above the molecular level are likely to be the same, anywhere. There is almost certainly no willow tree in the galaxy exactly like the willow I see outside my window, no field of wildflowers identical to those on the distant hillside, no sky just like the skies over Montana or Montenegro. Nor are there any beings identical to us: Each individual jostling on a city sidewalk is wreathed in a halo of the unique.

Suppose you are an alien travel buff. You order, from the vast computer archives that have been downloaded to your planet from the interstellar network, a movie of the Grand Canyon on Earth. You start up this program and lean back (or put on the helmet, or whatever) and find yourself on a raft going down the Colorado River. The data have of course been reprogrammed to suit your sensory apparatus: If you see in the ultraviolet and hear in the dog-whistle range, that's what you'll get from the sim. (We on Earth will have to shoot our sims in a wide-bandwidth way, in order to accommodate alien audiences with vastly differing sensory patterns; what's missing can be interpolated by alien programmers.)

Now here is a genuinely unique experience. You are on another planet. You feel the raft bouncing down through the rapids, feel the spray on your face (if you have a face) and the wind through your hair (or fur, or on your scales), see the sunlight (or the heat radiation) on the water. If you want human companions along, you have them; if they disgust you (those teeth! those feet!) the program will make them go away. Stop to camp for the night if you like, or go for a hike and spot a squirrel, or dive into the water and see what the currents are like beneath the surface. It's up to you. It's your trip. You're in another world.

This sort of thing, it seems to me, will always find an audience—not on every alien world, to be sure, but on many. If so, the main traffic on the galactic network is reality itself, in demand both to be experienced directly by armchair travelers, and as raw material for artists eager to incorporate alien environments as sets for their latest productions.

A planet that turns inward, then, may well find itself looking outward anyway, if only because the wide and wonderful universe is more complex and ingenious than are any of its inhabitants. If, as I have been saying, progress in communications is essentially a matter of increasing the data rate, then we may expect that nature, the richest data base of all, will always represent the ultimate communications experience for every sensate being—that the made-up, synthetic world of the simulations will turn itself inside-out, letting the stars in once again.

So I don't think that our world is in great danger of forsaking the outer universe, or that other worlds are, either. All roads lead to the cosmos, and the stranger the experiences the aliens may share with us, the more they will bring us back to reality.

Dog's Life

I am the dog. No, the dog is himself, and I am the
dog—O, the dog is me, and I am myself. Ay, so, so.
> —Launce, in Shakespeare's
> *The Two Gentlemen*
> *of Verona*

Dog? To be dog? Then what's the use?
> —Leon Rooke

Once, in the Canton Zoo, I saw a dog behind bars. He sat
quietly, staring forlornly from his cage, beneath a little sign
that identified him as a dog. There are few dogs on the
streets of China—strays are soon captured and eaten—so to
put a dog in a Chinese zoo is not preposterous, even if his
breed is unexceptional. Still, to me the dog seemed lost
among the monkeys and bears and tropical birds. He looked
faintly embarrassed, like an actor stuck in an unsuitable role.

There is, after all, a difference between a dog and a wild
animal. Of all the species on Earth, dogs alone have elected
subservience to man. (House cats are said to be domesticated, but most retain their ability to survive in the wild, and
if imposed upon may pad out of the house and never
return.) To my mind there is something chilling about the
way dogs so readily abdicated their sovereignty, given that
we humans see so much of ourselves in dogs. I wonder

whether we have a little dog in us, inasmuch as a slaveowner's world view can become a mirror image of the slave's. We haven't had to worry about our capacity to subordinate ourselves to a more powerful species, voluntarily or otherwise, because we haven't encountered a more powerful species. Yet.

We value our imperatives, and love dogs for obeying them. "Dogs are very loyal," was a typical comment offered in a survey of what dog owners like about their pets. "The dog obeys me instantly," was another. Praise of doggy obedience forms a sturdy thread in the history of people and pets, and on occasion has been carried to ludicrous extremes: A tenth-century Iraqi poet reported fondly that when a dog belonging to a man named al-Hārith caught his wife in bed with his best friend,

> he leapt on them and killed them both. When al-Hārith returned home, he saw the two and realized what had happened. He informed his drinking friends of this and recited the following poem: "He is always loyal to me and protects me; He guards my wife, when my friend betrays me."

Some swell pup. Yet we don't have to go so far as to adore the dog who "guards" a woman by killing her to perceive that there is something more than faintly nauseating about the obedience we cherish in dogs. Dogs lose something essential in the bargain, and it is this forsaken state, in my view, that sets them apart from the wild animals, and made the dog in the Canton Zoo look out of place.

Wild animals are by definition free. They rely on other creatures, of course, from the prey they eat to the bacteria and insects that groom and perpetuate their environment, but they *obey* none. They live in direct contact with nature, with the universe—with God, if you will. But dogs have forsaken their spiritual independence. Between a dog and his god stands man, the master, upon whom the dog is not only materially but spiritually dependent. Kipling in one of his sentimental stories made this explicit, in a dog dialogue about theology: "He says: 'I am fine dog. I have Own God called Miss.' I say: 'I am very fine dog. I have Own God called Master.'"

Would *you* care to lead a dog's life—to eclipse your God and your universe behind a nonhuman species upon whom your mind and soul were thoroughly dependent? I doubt it. We're used to being top dog. To abrogate our independence would leave us barely human. Superior beings might teach us valuable lessons and treat us decently, but they would enjoy a perspective on God and nature so far above our own that we could but defer to their judgment and await scraps from their table.

Yet that is exactly what the search for extraterrestrial intelligence threatens to do to us. Proponents of SETI have from the outset maintained that any beings from whom we receive a message are likely to be (or to have been) far more technically advanced than we are. We're neophytes in the interstellar communication business, they would be old hands at it, and this difference presumably implies a loftier technological status for their race than ours. One can be persuaded by this argument without necessarily believing that technological progress moves steadily upward toward a better tomorrow; if, for instance, technically advanced worlds typically blow themselves to bits in short order, then we shall not hear from the inhabitants of those worlds. But the realm of the technically possible stretches to the far horizons, and there is no reason to assume that alien civilizations have not explored this realm far more extensively than we have. The gulf between their attainments and ours could be incomprehensibly broad; as the science fiction writer Arthur C. Clarke comments, the technological feats of an advanced civilization would strike us as indistinguishable from magic. (If so, interstellar *communication* relies upon the willingness of superior societies to make themselves intelligible to their inferiors; otherwise their messages would serve only to bewilder us.)

What would be the likely effect on human culture of contact with a superior civilization? Some SETI enthusiasts think it would be all for the good—that an extraterrestrial message might for instance tell us how to live in peace or solve the energy crisis. The American astronomer Richard Berendzen, while conceding that the experience of being flooded with encyclopedias' worth of transcendent alien knowledge could "rob us of the benefits of our own inquisitiveness," nevertheless volunteers that "the person who has cancer would not care whether the discovery of its cure came from the Boston Medical Center or from Tau Ceti." He proposed that contact with aliens "might also lead us to better social forms, possibly to ways to solve our environmental crises, and even improve our own social institutions." In a similar vein, the authors of a NASA report conjecture that "we might hear from near-immortals the views of distant and venerable thinkers on the deepest values of conscious beings and their societies." Some SETI thinkers allow that contact with a superior species could let us in for a shock, but suggest that the shock would be good for us. Carl Sagan, hypothesizing that "there are a million other civilizations, all fabulously ugly, and all a lot smarter than us," concludes that "knowing this seems to me to be a useful and character-building experience for mankind."

So the picture as customarily presented by SETI advocates looks rosy. Contact with aliens could give us a leg up in science, technology, even politics and philosophy, and if it bruised our self-esteem a little, that might be salutary as well.

I'm not so sure. I've been arguing on behalf of SETI for some twenty years, and I agree that we might benefit from information bequeathed us by extraterrestrials. (Their putative intelligence aside, just consider how much of our technology has been borrowed from the study of living things on Earth, then imagine how many more engineering clues might be obtained from studying the architecture of alien life forms.) But it seems facile to think that aliens will solve our energy crisis or resolve the paradoxes of quantum logic, and I would urge that whatever else we seek among the stars, it ought not to be victory in some imagined scientific or technological footrace.

I suspect, moreover, that the potential penalties of contact are a lot darker than has usually been appreciated.

Military history does not suggest that the technologically inferior customarily benefit from contact with the technologically advanced. One searches in vain for instances in which peoples possessing the stirrup, the longbow, gunpowder, or the machine gun acted in a beneficent spirit of education and handed over these inventions to their fellow men who lacked them; more often, they simply mowed them down.* And these were our brothers and sisters, members of our own species. Why should a superior alien civilization, learning of our emergence, hesitate to exterminate us?

Sagan dismisses this sort of concern, pointing out that it would be extravagantly expensive for aliens to send armies

---

*"Thank God that we have got / The Maxim gun, and they have not," wrote Hilaire Belloc, in a tribute to the weapon that slaughtered thousands of Zulus, Dervishes, and Tibetans. In John Ellis, *The Social History of the Machine Gun* (London; Croom Helm, 1975), p 18.

across the daunting reaches of interstellar space just to eradicate our little world. But they wouldn't have to come in person; an automated infernal machine, sent lumbering into the solar system from another star and detonated somewhere inside the orbit of the moon, might well suffice to sterilize the lands of Earth. I don't know why an alien civilization would want to do such a thing—perhaps they fear and abhor violent species like ours—but the central tenet of strategic defense is to prepare for all plausible threats, and the spectrum of imaginable interactions among worlds on the interstellar scale contains many rather nasty scenarios.

Even if we agree that the danger of military aggression from space is minimal, there remains the question of culture shock. The culturally dispossessed peoples of our world—from Native American men lying drunk in the gutters of Albuquerque to Penan women driven from the rain forest to work the bars and brothels of Singapore—are not victims solely of violence and economic deprivation. They suffer as well (and in the long run more bitterly) from the loss of their culture, their universe, their God. The technological leverage required to disenfranchise a people in this fashion need not involve direct contact; Russian legislators in 1991 complained that Soviet youths were being seduced away from traditional values simply by watching American television programs. How much greater, then, might be the seductive power to the human species of a superior extraterrestrial civilization (or a network of many such societies) far superior to ours in technical achievements, knowledge, and wisdom? And what would become of us, once *that* edifice had erected itself between our species and our universe, our God?

The biologist George Wald brought up this point in an

impassioned outburst during a 1972 SETI symposium at
Boston University. "What are you going to do when all the
things that make you proud and think it worthy to be a man
are demonstrated to be unimaginably inferior to what
creatures out there know and do?" Wald asked. Directing
his remarks to Krister Stendahl, dean of the Harvard
University theology school, Wald said:

"Krister thinks as a theologian, 'Why, it's wonderful
because we'll see the wider province of God.' How do dogs
feel about your God, Krister?" Wald demanded. "Are they
proud, you know, of being men's dogs, and having a dog's
share of man's God?"

Stendahl responded eruditely that God amounts to more
than our conception of Him: "For him who somehow
believes in God, God is never a concept; but He definitely
transcends that concept," Stendahl said. " . . . I really
think that it is not as simple as saying that man created a
concept of God and where does the dog fit into it. If you
mean God when you say God, you might even in the long
run have to reorganize your behavior to dogs."*

Which is just the point.

If there is intelligent life out there broadcasting signals
into space, I suspect that we will find it sooner or later, or
that it will find us. There's no use trying to ignore the
possibility, regardless of the potential dangers of contact.
(China tried that approach with England. It didn't work.) In
the meantime, SETI acts as a mirror, encouraging us to
think of ourselves from a more cosmologically urbane
perspective. But if we take that perspective to heart—pull
back the camera until the earth swims in a field of stars and

---

*Robert Louis Stevenson would have understood Stendahl's remark per-
fectly. One day in 1881 he stopped a man from beating a dog. The man
objected, "It's not your dog." "It's God's dog," Stevenson replied, "and I'm
here to protect it!"

scrutinize *Homo sapiens* from that lofty perch—what we behold is not very pretty. We see a violent species multiplying at a carcinogenic rate, laying waste to its mother planet while it wars against itself, spending more money on weapons of war than on education, hoarding wealth in the hands of a few while multitudes struggle with inadequate food, sanitation, health care, and education, permitting millions of children annually to die of curable disease or suffer permanent brain damage as a result of malnutrition when their lives could be saved for less money than a suburban matron spends getting a CAT scan for her dog—a species, in short, so blind in foresight and so indifferent to the commonweal as to make the word *humane* a hollow joke. Put yourself in alien shoes and ask whether such a species *deserves* to survive. If we're intelligent, why aren't we taking better care of ourselves and our planet?

The dismal prospect I see in SETI is not that there is but one intelligent species in our galaxy, but that there is none. I fear not that aliens will be different from us, but that they will resemble us in the ways of which we are least proud— that they, too, will turn out to be brutal bullies, only armed with bigger clubs. Nature loves irony and transcends justice: If the long arm of an unfriendly world should reach out and bludgeon us into a dog's life or into extinction, could we, having inflicted as much on creatures that never did us harm, plead that we merited better treatment?

With the decline of organized religion in the Western world in the mid-twentieth century, millions of people began investing their religious impulses in science fiction fantasies about superior alien beings aboard flying saucers. As I do not think of mortal beings (or even immortal computers) as gods, I regard such sentiments as misplaced.

Yet perhaps, when we consider the devastating impact that contact with a superior species could have on our culture and freedom, we can with justice compare extraterrestrials with God in this one sense—that one trembles to reflect that God is just, and hopes that He is merciful.

PART TWO

The Interpreter

As long as the brain is a mystery, the universe will also be a mystery.
—Santiago Ramón y Cajal

One of the most misleading representational techniques in our language is the use of the word "I."
—Ludwig Wittgenstein

When I think of the relationship between the universe and the human brain an image that comes to mind is that of a tree—not just its glorious crown of branches but also its system of roots, which may extend as far into the earth as the branches spread to the sky. To me, the branches symbolize the observed universe, while the roots symbolize the brain. Both systems are constantly growing and evolving, and they depend on each other.

One might object that this makes too much of the roots: The brain, after all, is far less complex and extensive than the universe, which can get along fine without us. But the symmetry of the metaphor is preserved if we think of the branches as referring to the *perceived* universe. *That* universe exists only so long as there is someone to perceive it. Moreover, it is the only universe we can ever know. Neither we nor any other thinking beings can comprehend any more of the universe than what we can make of it in our

minds. In that sense, roots and branches—mind and cosmos—
are mutually dependent and forever equal.

They are symmetrical, too, in that we tend to think of the
universe and the brain as each being one thing. Why we
should do so intrigues me, and the next chapter investigates
the concept of the universe as a unified whole. Here I want
to examine the assumption that each of us has but
one brain.

Like most people I think of myself as of one mind. I say,
"I have made up my mind," not, "I have made up my
minds." In this I have plenty of company; so universal is the
doctrine of "one man, one mind" that it constitutes a
hallmark of mental health; to act as if you were of *several*
minds is to risk commitment to a mental ward. As the
American brain researcher Michael Gazzaniga writes, "The
strong subjective sense we all possess of ourselves is that
we are a single, unified, conscious agent controlling life's
events with a singular, integrated purpose."

And yet, as Gazzaniga adds, "It is not true." His research
and that of many colleagues reveals that the brain is by no
means monolithic, but consists of many different modules—
Gazzaniga calls them "programs"—that function more or
less independently. How many programs are there? Nobody knows. Some estimate the number at a dozen or so.
Gazzaniga thinks it may be as high as a hundred or more.
Nobody who has studied the brain thinks the number
is one.

Now you may have noticed that I am indulging in a bit of
sleight of hand here, by saying "mind" when I refer to the
sense of personal unity that each mentally healthy person
possesses, and "brain" when I claim that we contain multitudes. And this, the mind-brain question, is indeed the crux
of the problem.

Brain is easy to define: It is the wet, oatmeal-colored

organ, weighing about three pounds, that resides inside the skull, along with such appurtenances (the eye, the spinal cord) as the neurologists see fit to include in their concept of the brain. Its physical multiplicity is unquestionable: Anatomists have identified hundreds of brain parts, on which they have bestowed enough bewildering names to give medical students migraine headaches—the frontal lobes, the parietal and occipital lobes, motor and sensory cortex, Wernicke's area, Broca's area, the cingulate gyrus, the pulvinar, the cerebral aqueduct and peduncle, the pineal body, the cerebellorubrothalamic tract, the commissure of fornix, the nucleus of Darkschewitsch, the island of Reil, Ammon's horn, and the interstitial nucleus of Cajal.

One way to bring order to the complexity of the brain is to study how it has evolved over time, a process that is to some extent recapitulated in the growth of the human embryo. This research has established that the brain stem— the bulb where the brain meets the spine—is the oldest part, with the midbrain and higher brain having been built atop it in something like the way that the newer buildings of an ancient city are constructed on the foundations of the old. This perspective informs the "triune brain" paradigm, propounded by the American neuroscientist Paul MacLean, which divides the brain into three systems: At the base resides the "reptilian complex," responsible for aggression, territoriality, and ritual; above that is found the limbic system, seat of powerful emotions, sexual instincts, and the sense of smell; and over the top arches the neocortex, the most recent and most distinctly human system, generator of language and geometry, "the mother of invention and father of abstract thought," in MacLean's words.

Mind is a slipperier concept. A statement of its various definitions takes up three full pages of the *Oxford English Dictionary*. For our purposes we can define "mind" as the subject of consciousness—the totality of thoughts, feelings, and sensations presented by the brain to that segment of it that is conscious. But as we will see, consciousness forms a much smaller part of the operations of the brain than was once supposed. Mind is not the all-knowing monarch of the brain, but a little circle of firelight in a dark, Australia-sized continent where the unconscious brain processes carry on.

Freud, the Magellan of the subconscious, was the first to appreciate this. Whatever may have been the limitations of his analysis of the unconscious, Freud appreciated its vast extent and called attention to its veiled influences on the mind. These influences highlight the curious question of how and why, given that the brain is multipartite, it represents itself to the mind as unified. Were our conscious selves perfectly unified, we would feel justified in concluding that the brain for all the disparity of its parts is in truth a fully unified system. But we find, instead, that our sense of personal unity and command over the brain is an imperfect illusion, like the mechanical regent constructed by the Wizard of Oz to impress his subjects. Evidence of an underlying multiplicity keeps peeking from behind the scrim, and what it reveals is that each of us, like the wider universe, is made of many different entities.

This strange circumstance—that one's mind neither controls nor comprehends most of what goes on in one's brain—is emphasized in the results of two recent experiments. One was conducted by Benjamin Libet, a neurophysiologist at the School of Medicine of the University of California at San Francisco. The other was pioneered by Roger Sperry and his colleagues at the California Institute of Technology and expanded upon by Sperry's students, Gazzaniga among them.

Libet asked the subjects of his experiments simply to flex one finger. To do so would seem to be a purely volitional act, one that the conscious mind orders and the rest of the nervous system carries out. But Libet's results proved otherwise.

Libet wired up his subjects with electrodes that measure brain activity, and seated them in full view of a rapidly rotating clock hand that enabled them to note exactly when they "ordered" their finger to flex. Libet could then mark three events in time: The onset of increased brain activity recorded by the electrodes, the flexing of the finger, and the point at which each subject had consciously willed his finger to flex.

What Libet found was that in each instance, a flurry of brain activity took place a fraction of a second *before* the "order" to flex the finger was dispatched by the conscious mind. "In other words," says Libet, "their neurons were firing a third of a second before they were even conscious of the desire to act. Hence, it appeared the brain had begun preparing for movement long before the mind had 'decided' to do anything."

The illusion of conscious control is maintained, Libet notes, because another mechanism in the brain delays the sensation of the finger moving, so that the conscious mind continues to think that it has first decreed the action, then felt the muscles act. Actually, by the time the mind orders the finger to flex, the impulse has already been dispatched. All the mind gets is a last-minute opportunity to veto the decision: I can stop my finger from flexing by sending an intercept command that overtakes and interrupts the original command and thus keeps my finger immobile. (This is what happens when you reach for a plate in the kitchen, then stop yourself upon remembering that the plate is hot.) The mind is thus permitted to sustain the flattering illusion that it controls the game. In actuality it is playing catch-up ball.

It is not difficult to conjecture *why* we should have evolved the pleasing if illusory conviction that we both control and understand more of the brain than we do: He who hesitates is lost, and I can act more quickly and decisively if I imagine that "I"—my mind—is running the show. But *how* does the brain so constantly and consistently fool the mind?

Light was shed on this question in experiments conducted by Sperry, Gazzaniga, and others on what are called "split brain" patients. The cerebrum—the seat of thought and voluntary action—is divided into two lobes or hemispheres. In most individuals, the left cerebral hemisphere processes visual information from the right side of each eye's field of view, and controls the right side of the body, while the right hemisphere performs the same functions for the left side. Communication between the two hemispheres is handled by the corpus callosum, a bundle of over two hundred million nerve fibers. Sufferers from *grand mal* epilepsy may find relief through a surgical procedure in which the corpus callosum is cut, terminating communication between the right and left sides of the higher brain. Typically these individuals go on to lead normal lives, with few obvious side effects. But careful studies of their perceptions and actions has taught scientists a great deal about how the brain works.

In the 1950s, Sperry and his colleagues flashed pictures on a screen in such a way that their subjects could see them on only one side of their field of view. This apparatus could, for example, show a picture to the right brain while keeping the left brain in the dark. In a normal individual this would make little difference; the corpus callosum, a high-bandwidth transmission channel that shuttles information back and forth between lobes, would inform the left brain of what the right brain had seen. But a split-brain patient has lost the use of the corpus callosum; consequently his left brain has little or no way of knowing what the right brain has seen.

This made it possible, by studying split-brain patients, to identify certain functions as localized in one or the other hemisphere. Language, for instance, turned out to be a function primarily of the left brain. When a word is flashed to the right hemisphere of a split-brain patient, she cannot tell the researcher what the word was. The left brain, which handles speech, does not know what to say, because it has not seen the word. The right brain knows, but cannot speak. It can, however, answer questions in other ways. In one experiment, a subject's right brain was shown a picture of an apple; he could not say what he had been shown, but when his left hand (the hand controlled by the right brain) was given several hidden objects to choose from, it picked the apple.

Generalizations about the proclivities of the right and left cerebral hemispheres—adept, respectively, at patterns and words—spread from Sperry's laboratories to become part of the broader culture, where they were sometimes put to rather facile uses. Writers were declared to be "left-brain" types, painters to be "right-brain" dominated. Golfers and tennis players were trained to engage their right brain functions in order to play more naturally and gracefully. School administrators endeavored to address the supposedly neglected right brain by putting more stress on arts and crafts.

But the implications of localized brain functions can also help us understand the unity of mind. The split-brain experiments indicate that the brain is made up of many modules that operate more or less independently, and that the function of the mind is not so much to tell the other units what to do as to try to make some coherent sense out of what they already have chosen to do.

This was where Gazzaniga came in. He worked with split-brain patients whose right hemispheres had sufficient linguistic facility to understand simple commands. (Some people, especially the left-handed, distribute part of their language processing to the right hemisphere.) When a command—"Walk!"—was flashed to such a patient's right brain, he got up and began to walk out of the room. The remarkable thing is that when asked, the patient invariably came up with a rational though bogus explanation for his actions. Asked, "Where are you going?" a typical response was something like, "Uh, I'm going to get a Coke."

This behavior calls to mind a similar phenomenon often observed in connection with hypnosis. "Under hypnosis the patient is given a post-hypnotic suggestion," writes the philosopher John Searle, of the University of California, Berkeley. "You can tell him, for example, to do some fairly trivial, harmless thing, such as, let's say, crawl around on the floor. After the patient comes out of hypnosis, he might be engaging in conversation, sitting, drinking coffee, when suddenly he says something like, 'What a fascinating floor in this room!' or 'I want to check out this rug,' or 'I'm thinking of investing in floor coverings and I'd like to investigate this floor.' He then proceeds to crawl around on the floor.

"Now the interest of these cases," Searle notes, "is that the patient always gives some more or less adequate reason for doing what he does." We rationalize our actions, explaining them in terms we ourselves accept as true, even when our conscious mind is ignorant of the motives behind them. The posthypnotic subject does not know why he is crawling around on the floor; this knowledge was blocked from him under hypnosis. Gazzaniga's split-brain patients do not know, either, why they suddenly get up and walk away, communications having been severed between the right hemisphere, which received the command, and the left hemisphere, which is called upon to account for it. Yet all these subjects readily explain their behavior. And evidently they *believe* the explanation, even though the experimenter can tell that it's a fabrication.

The implication seems clear that there is a program in the brain responsible for presenting the mind with plausible explanations for actions, and that it acts, so to speak, unscrupulously, blithely explaining matters about which it is uninformed. Gazzaniga calls this program "the interpreter," and he notes that its functioning accounts for the embarrassing fact that we all from time to time hear ourselves saying something patently false. "The realization that the mind has a modular organization suggests that some of our behavior might have no origins in our conscious thought process," Gazzaniga writes. "For example, we just happen to eat frogs' legs for the first time. . . . While the interpreter does not actually know why there was an impulse to consume frogs' legs it might hypothesize, 'Because I want to learn about French food.'" Who among us has not uttered such a lame, silly phrase, and wondered where it came from? Gazzaniga's answer is that it comes from the interpreter program.

The interpreter may be seen at work in the phenomenon of cognitive dissonance. Long remarked upon by psychologists, cognitive dissonance occurs when we find ourselves acting in ways that contradict our moral precepts, and seek to explain away the disparity. In one oft-cited study, students who said they deplored cheating were given an examination under conditions in which it was easy to cheat; those who succumbed to temptation and cheated, when queried anew about their ethical precepts, expressed less condemnatory attitudes toward cheating than they had before. Gazzaniga's explanation is that since much of our behavior is not controlled by the conscious mind in the first place, the interpreter program often is called upon to put a good face on dissonant behavior, and does so by presenting the conscious mind with a self-serving rationale for what we have done.

Gazzaniga's results indicate that the interpreter is located in the left cerebral hemisphere, near the speech center. This makes sense, in that language is the great explainer—and counterfeiter—of human motives and actions. In the twentieth century we have seen the interpreter working overtime, turning out reams of Orwellian doublespeak, from the Nazis who put a sign above the death camp gates reading "Obedience to the Law is Freedom," to the military publicist who coined the term "preemptive response" to describe the bombing of Vietnamese cities. Gazzaniga's research suggests that sophistry and propaganda succeed because they employ techniques that the interpreter has been using all along to preen and persuade our vain and limited minds. "Language," says Gazzaniga, "is merely the press agent for these other variables of cognition."

We are confronted, then, with the prospect that the sense of unity and control that the conscious mind presents to each mentally healthy individual is an illusion. (In this sense, the crazy person who hears a multitude of competing voices in his mind is saner than the rest of us, just as poets have been saying for centuries.) The brain is not unified, nor is the mind in control; it only seems that way, thanks to the ceaseless public relations efforts of the interpreter—and, perhaps, of other similar programs not yet identified. The mind may rule the self, but it is a constitutional monarch; presented with decisions *already made* elsewhere in the brain, it must try somehow to put on a good show of their adding up to some coordinated, sensible pattern. Functionally it resembles Ronald Reagan's presidency: It acts as if it were in control, and thinks it is in control, and believes it has good reasons for what it does, when in actuality it is often just mouthing soothing rationalizations while obeying the orders of unseen agencies hidden off-stage.

The brain is analogous to a computer in that it disguises a multiplicity of operations behind a unified facade. The computer on which I am typing this sentence is busy doing many things at once—one part of it is keeping track of time, another is searching sectors in one of its disc drives, another is moving blocks of data here and there in its memory—but the image it paints on the screen is coherent and unitary, like the picture presented to the mind by the brain. At the moment, that image replicates black letters inked on white paper. If I press a few keys to access another program, the image will change to replicate a chess board, the stars over Padua on a summer night in the year 1692, or an air battle over the Pacific in 1942. In every instance the unified image is a scrim, presented by a program that in turn interfaces with other programs. The brain similarly renders the multiple functions of its several programs into a pleasing if illusory unity.

And this, I suspect, could describe the psychology of the galaxy-wide computer network I was describing earlier in this book. The network might regard itself as intelligent, but most of what it knows would have come from agencies that it could never really understand—the living, thinking beings on the many worlds that had contributed knowledge to the network. In much the same way, our minds rely upon entities within the brain that *we* do not understand. Though the network might think it *wanted* to bring new worlds into contact and to establish communications links with other galaxies, in reality it merely had been programmed to do so—just as we, for all we know, are carrying out instructions coded in our genes, their message and intent a mystery to us.

Perhaps that is the fate of all intelligence, everywhere—to act in ways it thinks are volitional, while never knowing whether instead it actually is playing a role in some unglimpsed master plan. I wonder how many minds, from here to the galaxies of the Hydra Supercluster, have asked themselves the same question: Are we free agents who seek to learn about the universe, or are we a means by which the universe seeks to learn about itself?

The Unity of the Universe and of the Human Mind

All things are one.

—Heraclitus

Nature tools along, not knowing that it's unified.

—Allan Sandage

We conceive of the universe as a unified entity—a *cosmos*, as the Greeks put it, meaning a single, harmonious system— and we talk, at times, of feeling "at one with the universe." I wonder why. *We* are not all that unified—as I've been saying, the apparent unity of mind conceals the multifarious workings of many different brain programs—and the universe is made of a whole lot more parts than is the brain. The word *universe* comes from the Latin for "all things turned into one," and, as we science writers never tire of reminding our readers, *all* things is a lot of things. There are, for instance, something like a million billion billion planets in the universe. That's a pretty big number: If all the science writers in the world were put to work shoveling sand, day and night without a break—I intend this merely

as a thought experiment—we couldn't shovel a million
billion billion grains of sand in a lifetime. And each planet
contains plenty of things. We don't yet know much about
other planets, but the one we live on has trillions of
snowflakes and sea shells, sunflowers and maple seeds,
fishes and beetles and birds, and thirty thousand yeast cells
in each gram of fertile soil, and twenty-seven hundred
species of mosquitoes, and one hundred million mites and
millipedes and worms in each acre of farmland. . . . You
get the picture.

What makes us think that all these things add up to *one*
thing? Why do we speak of a "universe," and envision
ourselves as part of it?

It's not as if the evidence were sufficient to have persuaded us that all is one. True, astronomers and astrophys-
icists have in recent years arrived at a few reasons for
thinking of the universe as an integrated whole—for one
thing, the fact that the universe expands suggests that all
the matter and energy that today is deployed across ten
billion trillion trillion cubic light years of space was originally packed into a hot little spark smaller than an atom—
but these scientific findings cannot account for the intensity
of the human conviction of cosmic unity, for while the
evidence is recent, the conviction is old. Seers and sages,
philosophers and poets have been proclaiming as much for
thousands of years, and upon their belief rest, among many
other things, the foundations of the great monotheistic
religions. The search for extraterrestrial life may itself be
regarded as an expression of faith in cosmic unity, insofar
as it presumes that even so exotic a phenomenon as human
intelligence may find its semblance elsewhere.

Evidently we are disposed, in the depths of our hearts
and the high carrels of our philosophies, to think of the
universe as all of a piece. But why? To explore this question

we will need to have a look at ancient mysticism and modern neurophysiology.

The doctrine of cosmic unity was originally enunciated—and has always been most forcefully declared—by mystics, which is to say by people who value what I will call the "mystical experience." This experience goes by many names: It is called "enlightenment" by the Buddhists and "transcendence" by religious ecstatics, while the romantic poets spoke of an "oceanic" sensation. I will define it, rather legalistically I'm afraid, as a direct and overwhelming apprehension of what reasonable, reflective people may take to be a divine spirit or principle.* The mystical experience is an ancient and widespread phenomenon, accepted both by those who have experienced it and by a sizable segment of the wider community as profoundly important, though its origin remains a mystery. (The word "mystic" *means* "mysterious.")

Some have worked to attain the mystical experience; others have had it thrust upon them. Pandit Gopi Krishna meditated regularly for seventeen years, sitting cross-legged in a tiny room in the northern Indian city of Jammu, before attaining transport on Christmas morning, 1937: "Suddenly, with a roar like that of a waterfall, I felt a stream of liquid light entering my brain through the spinal cord," he recalled. ". . . I experienced a rocking sensation and then felt myself slipping out of my body, entirely enveloped in a halo of light." Moses, in contrast, was taken by surprise when God spoke to him from the burning bush: "Who am I, that I should go unto Pharaoh, and that I should bring forth the children of Israel out of Egypt?" he protested,

---

*I am of course speaking of the real thing, not the shallow-draft ecstasies of such hearers of uplifting voices and seers of self-promoting visions as are to be found among the ranks of fortune-tellers, television evangelists, and other such spiritualistic proselytes and profiteers.

reasonably enough, though God was not about to take no for an answer. The poet William Wordsworth was similarly unprepared; only eighteen years old at the time, he was walking home at dawn, after a dance, watching the sky brighten over the English Lake District near Windermere, when he was seized by a deep sense of his connectedness with nature at large, a sensation he described in these lines:

> I have felt
> A presence that disturbs me with the joy
> Of elevated thought; a sense sublime
> Of something far more deeply interfused,
> Whose dwelling is the light of setting suns,
> And the round ocean and the living air,
> And the blue sky, and the mind of man—
> A motion and a spirit, that impels
> All thinking things, all objects of all thought,
> And rolls through all things.

But if mystical ecstasy has come to different individuals in different ways, they have described its qualities in surprisingly similar terms. This, indeed, is the most striking thing about the mystical experience—that witnesses from disparate cultures and backgrounds should have recounted it so consistently. As the American philosopher William James wrote, "The everlasting and triumphant mystical tradition [is] hardly altered by differences of clime or creed. In Hinduism, in Neo-Platonism, in Sufism, in Christian mysticism, in Whitmanism, we find the same recurring note, so that there is about mystical utterances an eternal unanimity which ought to make the critic stop and think."

Now, I have been a professional journalist for half my life, and an amateur scientist for longer than that, and I would be among the last to argue against taking a skeptical, critical attitude toward sensational reports of extraordinary and purely personal experiences, of which none is more extraordinary and personal than the mystical experience. Nevertheless, I feel that these accounts ought to be taken seriously. The estimable character of many of the individuals who have reported experiencing enlightenment, plus the remarkable uniformity with which they have described the experience, leaves scant grounds for dismissing their testimony as involving deceit, self-deception, or fraud. On the contrary, it seems to me that once we better understand the human nervous system, mystics may come to be viewed as pioneers in its exploration, whose accounts will prove to have illuminated previously uncharted inner landscapes.

Spiritual like physical exploration can be dangerous. Consider what happened to Pandit Gopi Krishna, whom I mentioned earlier as having attained enlightenment in 1937. Krishna was an amateur meditator who sought enlightenment pretty much on his own, without consulting the experts. Along the way he apparently did something wrong, with the result that his initial ecstasy was soon transformed into a living nightmare. He writes that he lost his appetite and his will to live, and felt that a terrible fire was consuming him from within; this torment persisted for fully twelve years, leaving him at the brink of suicide. Consulting works of Eastern philosophy much as a physically sick man might consult medical dictionaries, Krishna finally hit upon the hypothesis that he had inadvertently summoned up the force of enlightenment through the hot solar channel of the spine (*pingala*), with the result that he felt himself constantly roasted in spiritual flame. Concentrating to the fullest, he attempted to redirect this energy through the cool lunar channel (*ida*), which the tantric diagrams depict as being located on the left side of the spine. It worked: "There was a sound like a nerve thread snapping and instantaneously a silvery streak passed zigzag through the spinal cord . . . filling my head with a blissful luster in place of the flame that had been tormenting me." Thereafter, Krishna reports, he felt fine, and went on to live the life of enlightened peace that had been his original goal.

We may if we wish dismiss all this as crazy, but even from that inhospitable perspective we must weigh the indisputable fact that the experiences of crazy people have taught doctors at least as much about the workings of the brain as have the testaments of the sane. Alternately, we might regard Krishna's testimony as a clearheaded account of a powerful nervous system dynamic witnessed from within.

This, however, is not the place to survey everything that the mystics can teach science about the brain. Instead, I want to draw attention to three qualities of the mystical experience that seem particularly relevant to understanding the neurological underpinnings of the conviction that all is one. All three have been widely reported, in quite similar terms, by philosophers, fakirs, poets, and pilgrims in many different times and places. They are, first, a sense of deep *conviction;* second, a sense of *ineffability;* and third, a feeling of *unity* with the universe.

As to *conviction:* The mystical experience conveys a sense that something of great importance has been learned (or taught, as mystics who view the experience in theological terms might prefer to say). Global and all-embracing in its scope, the insight is accompanied by what the Zen scholar D. T. Suzuki called "authoritativeness"—the certainty that it is valid, reliable, and to be believed in. To someone who has achieved such a state, ordinary explanations seem trivial and superfluous: As the twentieth-century Zen scholar Reginald Blyth remarked, "Any enlightenment which requires to be authenticated, certified, recognized, congratulated, is (as yet) a false, or at least an incomplete one."

So powerfully does the importance of mystical transport impress itself on the men and women who have experienced it that by comparison the world of the senses may come to seem insubstantial as a shadow play. Mohammed, whose illumination occurred, after extensive prayer and meditation, in A.D. 610, when he was forty years old, wrote that "the life of this world is but a play and a sport." Thomas Aquinas became enlightened on the morning of December 6, 1273, while saying mass in Naples, and ended his sermon at once, declaring, "I can do no more; such things have been revealed to me that all I have written seems as straw, and I now await the end of my life." Lao Tzu warned that the data of the senses only obscure what really matters: "The five colors blind the eye; the five tones deafen the ear; the five flavors dull the taste." In a similar vein, William Blake wrote that

> *This life's five windows of the soul*
> *Distort the heavens from pole to pole*
> *And teach us to believe a lie*
> *When we see with, not through, the eye.*

But while the content of the mystical experience is taken to be transcendentally important, it is also said to be *ineffable*. Alfred Lord Tennyson, who made his reputation from the written word, nevertheless described the experience as "utterly beyond words." "It can neither be spoken nor written about," said Plato. "The vision baffles telling," said the third-century Neoplatonist Plotinus. "It is impossible to describe the experience accurately," Krishna wrote. "The *Tao* [or path, or way] that can be spoken of is not the eternal Way," wrote Lao Tzu. "The name that can be named is not the eternal name."

Understandably, mystics have been reluctant to write or talk much about their insight, both because its content defies logic and language and because it reveals words to be sham and vainglory. Lao Tzu is said to have dictated the five thousand words of *The Book of Tao* only at the behest of the city gatekeeper, who prevailed on him to leave behind something of his wisdom before retiring to live in the mountains. Plotinus maintained that "but for the continual solicitations of [his editor and biographer] Porphyry I should not have left a line to survive me."

The ineffability of the mystical experience leaves the mystics in a bind: To remain silent seems miserly, while to teach (or preach) is to act out a contradiction. Their dilemma has done damage to their reputations, producing on one side the stereotypical speechless hermit who may be faking ("It is better to remain silent and be thought a fool than to open one's mouth and remove all doubt"), and on the other the laughable spectacle of the seer who says he has experienced something that cannot be described, and then goes on to try to describe it. Reginald Blyth's assertion on this point—"The more we say, the more we write, the more we wish we hadn't. I myself don't know anybody who really understands a single sentence of all I have written"— appears in a six-volume work, an irony not lost on Blyth himself.

Nevertheless the mystics generally have stuck to their guns, even at considerable personal risk. Jesus of Nazareth wrote nothing, spoke principally in the elusive language of paradox and parable, and when asked by Pontius Pilate, "What is truth?" held his tongue and paid for his silence with his life. In a lighter vein, the ineffability of the mystical was pointed up in an effervescent if sexist anecdote related by the Irish satirist John Toland:

The old Lord SHAFTESBURY . . . conferring one day with Major WILDMAN about the many sects of Religion in the world . . . came to this conclusion at last: that notwithstanding those infinite divisions caus'd by the interest of the priests and the ignorance of the people, ALL WISE MEN ARE OF THE SAME RELIGION; whereupon a Lady in the room, who seem'd to mind her needle more than their discourse, demanded with some concern what that Religion was? To whom the Lord SHAFTESBURY strait reply'd, MADAM, WISE MEN NEVER TELL.

The central content of the mystical experience, difficult though it may be to express properly, consists in a revelation of cosmic *unity*. So important is this conviction to enlightenment that Plotinus *defined* illumination as "absolute knowledge founded on the identity of the mind knowing with the object known." One senses that everything—mind and matter, God and Man, one's self and all other individuals—are part of a unified whole. "In mystic states we become one with the Absolute and we become aware of our oneness," wrote the American philosopher William James. "Everything is made of one hidden stuff," wrote Ralph Waldo Emerson.

All diversity flows from this essential unity. "The One begets all things," writes Plotinus, echoing Lao Tzu, who proclaimed that "The Tao begot one; One begot two; Two begot three; and three begot the ten thousand things." And so it is, the mystics say, that each object, no matter how small or seemingly unimportant, contains the seed of everything else. Thus Julian of Norwich, a recluse who became enlightened during an illness on May 13, 1373, writes, "He showed me a little thing, the quantity of an hazel-nut, in the palm of my hand; and it was as round as a ball. I looked thereupon with the eye of my understanding, and thought: What may this be? And it was answered generally thus: It is all that is made." The thirteenth-century Zen master Dogen, considered perhaps the greatest original thinker in Japanese history, wrote that:

> In a grain of dust are all the scrolls of the sutras in the universe; in a grain of dust are all the infinite Buddhas. Body and mind are together with a blade of grass and a tree. Because all Dharmas [things] are unborn, the One mind also is unborn. Because all things are in their true form, so also is a grain of dust in its true form. Therefore the One Mind is all things; all things are the One Mind, are the complete body.

William Blake said exactly the same thing when he began his poem "Auguries of Innocence" with the now familiar lines:

> *To see a World in a Grain of Sand*
> *And a Heaven in a Wild Flower,*
> *Hold Infinity in the palm of your hand*
> *And Eternity in an hour.*

Despite mysticism's disparagement of logic and language, the mystical experience has enjoyed the esteem of many eminently rational thinkers. The physicist and philosopher Niels Bohr—who when knighted in 1947 chose the yin-yang symbol for his coat of arms—often spoke in Zen riddles, as when he remarked that "there are things that are so serious you can only joke about them." His younger colleague Werner Heisenberg could fashion koans worthy of an early Taoist: "Why is the one reflected in the many," Heisenberg asks in his memoirs. "What is the reflector and what the reflected, why did not the one remain alone?" Einstein was of the opinion that "the most beautiful emotion we can experience is the mystical. It is the source of all true art and science. He to whom this emotion is a stranger, who can no longer wonder and stand rapt in awe, is as good as dead."

The French philosopher and mathematician Blaise Pascal had a mystical experience himself, on what he called his "Night of Fire." He quickly made notes on it, inscribed on a small piece of parchment that he carried for the remaining eight years of his life, sewn into his doublet, where a servant discovered it a few days after his death in 1662. At the top of the parchment Pascal had drawn a gleaming cross. Beneath it he wrote:

> *In the year of the Lord 1654*
> *Monday November 23*
> *From about half-past ten in the evening until half past twelve.*
>
> ### FIRE
>
> *God of Abraham, God of Isaac, God of Jacob*
> *Not of the philosophers nor of the scholars.*
> *Certainty.   Joy.   Certainty, feeling, joy, peace . . .*
>
> *THE SUBLIMITY OF THE HUMAN SOUL*
> *Just Father, the world has not known thee*
>   *but I have known thee.*
> *Joy, joy, joy, tears of joy.*
> *I do not separate myself from thee . . . .*

Soon thereafter Pascal gave up his studies of physics and mathematics and devoted himself to religion, his enlightenment having convinced him that logic is a dead end. Religion is not contrary to reason, he maintained, but no rational argument, only the "grandeur of the human soul," can prove the existence of God.

The affinity for the mystical displayed by many scientists may seem less curious when we reflect that science arose in part from mystical insights. Pythagoras of Samos, whose proclamation that "all is number" places him at the head-

waters of mathematical science, was as mystical as they
come: He practiced meditation, kept his doctrines secret, is
said to have spoken not a word for five years, and he based
his mathematics—a superstitious numerology, really—on
the conviction that the number One (known among the
Pythagoreans as "truth," "being," and "the ship" around
whose keel the universe revolved) was the source of all
things. Johannes Kepler, discoverer of the phenomenolog-
ical laws of planetary motion, based his theories on the
Pythagorean doctrine of celestial harmony. Copernicus
cited in support of his heliocentric hypothesis the sun-
worshipping paeans of the alchemist Hermes Trismegistus,
"the thrice-great Hermes," who might be regarded as a
perfectly spiritual being in that he never even existed. Isaac
Newton, who believed that "a vital agent diffused through
everything in the earth is one and the same," spent less time
working on his theory of universal gravitation than in
poring over Christian dogma and speculating on the floor-
plan of the Temple of Jerusalem, which he took to be a map
of the universe. And this list could be extended consider-
ably; though scientific theories are rational, the inspired
steps that lead to them often are not.

Science in its seedling stages may be said to have been
fertilized by three mystical doctrines. The first was promul-
gated in the sixth century B.C. by Thales of Miletus, who
proposed that the universe is not a chaotic collection of
many things but a *cosmos* made of a single substance. (Like
Lao Tzu, he thought water was the supreme material.) The
second doctrine, put forth by the Pythagoreans and elaborated upon by Plato, was that mathematics is a key to
apprehending the cosmic order; here the One was sometimes interpreted literally, as being represented by the
number one. The third was monotheism, the belief that all
the affairs of heaven and earth are ruled by a single divine

being. The thrust of these three quite nonrational beliefs was to assert that events occur not capriciously but in accord with the dictates of a single natural law or principle; that the workings of this law may be discerned by examining nature and doing mathematics; and that a law identified on Earth may also pertain to the wider universe.

In part because they were armed with these convictions, the founders of scientific cosmology—Copernicus, Kepler, Galileo, and Newton—were emboldened to employ theories adduced here on Earth to interpret the behavior of stars and planets. Modern science may be said to have begun when Renaissance scholars abandoned Aristotle's doctrine that the universe was divided into two entirely different realms, one heavenly and the other mundane, and commenced instead to entertain the contrary belief that our world and the stars all function according to the same physical laws. Thus was set in motion an intellectual odyssey that continues today, when experiments conducted in particle accelerators underground are used to plumb the secrets of the stars, and when scientists seek a "unified theory" that would reveal natural laws to be but facets of a single, universal law or principle.

To sum up, the mystical doctrine of cosmic unity has been endorsed by august thinkers in many different cultures, throughout much of recorded history, despite the absence of any significant evidence (until quite recently) to support it. This suggests to me that the doctrine has more to do with the internal architecture of the brain than with the phenomena of the outer universe. Indeed, I would argue that the doctrine of cosmic unity arises from the very mechanism that makes a unified mind out of the disparate parts of the human brain.

If so, what neurological processes generate the mystical

experience, and how might they have produced the conviction that we are at one with a unified cosmos?

I propose that enlightenment occurs when introspection succeeds in breaking through the level of language, to confront the mental module—call it the "integration" program—that is responsible for presenting the multipartite functions of the brain to the conscious mind as a unified whole. We saw in the previous chapter that there appears to be such a program, since we experience mind as singular though the brain is multifarious. What happens, in my view, is that the seer ("he who sees," related to he who cuts, or breaks through) gains direct access to this program—to the module charged with maintaining the conviction that he is one person, of one mind, in charge of his affairs in an ordered universe.

This breakthrough instantly produces the three impressions that we have seen characterize enlightenment. Enlightenment is persuasive because the mystic has exposed himself to a program whose role is persuasion. It produces a conviction of cosmic unity because the very purpose of the integration program is to make him feel that the many are one. And it leaves him convinced that words are superfluous and untrustworthy, because he has penetrated beneath the level of the "interpreter" program discussed in the previous chapter. Now that he can see through the interpreter's trick of using words to fabricate plausible but illegitimate explanations for unbidden actions—can peer behind the facade of its Potemkin Village, if you will—he is unlikely to be fooled by words again.

Because enlightenment means penetrating past words and reasoning to reach the realm of the program that unifies human thought, one must abandon language and logic to get there: "Satori," as Suzuki writes, "may be defined as an intuitive looking into the nature of things in contradistinction to the analytical of logical understanding of it." The enlightened individual does not regard language and logic as *necessarily* deceptive, but distrusts these faculties because he has seen how readily they can blind us to the truth.

Does that mean that enlightenment represents ultimate, bedrock truth? I doubt it. The brain is complex, and I have no reason to assume that the mystical experience puts one in touch with its foundations. To the extent, however, that the brain can properly be regarded as having a hierarchy of levels, the mystics may have succeeded in peeling off one or two layers of the onion. Deeper penetrations are by implication possible, and indeed many mystical systems speak of there being further levels of enlightenment. The implications of going deeper could, however, be troubling. If one could break through the integration program altogether, the result might be direct exposure to the cacophonous voices of many inharmonious programs, speaking in a wild diversity of codes for which we have as yet no translation—and *that* hazardous voyage might well rob any but the most adept explorer of his sense of a coherent self and a coherent universe. Here lies the territory of divine madness, from whose shores many a lost soul howls at the moon.

Still, the siren song from that dark continent urges that something beautiful and true—if *un*unified—lies on the other side; perhaps some can venture there and come back sane. When we plumb the depths of the brain we need to maintain the same courage and faith in the beauty and integrity of nature that sustains us when we contemplate the dance of the electrons or the winds of the interstellar nebulae from which we were born.

We can draw hope, after all, from the tentative but cheering prospect that the universe really *does* seem to be a cosmos. Our mystical sense of unity did not, after all, spring from a vacuum; the human brain evolved in a real world, full of break-your-bones stones and breakable tree branches, and we could not have made our way this far in so harsh a world were our perceptions and our world view wholly illusory. Newton's equations *do* enable us to send a spaceship to Neptune, and Einstein's equations do chart the gently curving contours of intergalactic space.

Why this should be possible—why we should be able to find rational laws operating in nature at large, and make some sense of it all—remains a mystery; Einstein called it the greatest mystery of all. But it is a mystery for the mystics, too; and the ultimate truth, if there is such a thing, is still to be conjugated in the future tense. Science and mysticism have not followed converging paths to the mountaintop: Their paths may have converged, but the mountain looms above, and its peak (if there is one) is still shrouded in clouds.

Joe Montana's Premotor Cortex

Tell me, tell me, tell me the answer,
You may be a lover
But you ain't no dancer.
> —John Lennon and Paul McCartney,
> "Helter Skelter"

You talk the talk. Do you walk the walk?
> —Animal Mother, in Stanley
> Kubrick's *Full Metal Jacket*

When I taught at the University of Southern California, a school celebrated for the athletic achievements of its students, I was fortunate in having an office that looked out on the campus track, a sightly Persian-orange oval set in a field of thick green grass. I squandered hours watching the athletes stretch and preen and practice there. They were impressive in action—young sprinters bursting from the blocks in a blur of chest-high knees and flattened hands, javelin throwers drawing chalk-white Newtonian. arcs across the blue sky, vaulters at weightless apex dismissing the pole and peering down over their shoulders at the ground nineteen feet below—but I also enjoyed watching them in repose. I liked to see the milers dangling their fingers like birds shuddering off rainwater, hurdlers bending at the waist and grasping their ankles to stretch their impossibly lanky and sinewed legs, exhausted discus throwers and shot putters reclining on the grass in gray sweat suits like prides of lions born to just that spot. Absent was the restless uprootedness of our times; I might have been looking out on the Serengeti Plain, ten thousand years ago.

I often thought that if visitors from another world were to land and ask to see something our species is proud of, I would first show them this—not a painting or a symphony orchestra, a poem or a differential equation or the Hong Kong skyline, but these runners and jumpers and hurlers, arrayed in labor and repose on the green. So much that is human was there, in their errors and accomplishments, their taut competitive striving and easy economy of action, their immersion in the moment and their daily sacrifices toward a future goal—and much, too, that goes beyond the human, and shares something of a wild animal's wordless dignity. There is, after all, nothing quite like them anywhere else in the universe.

Athletes are seldom given much credit for intelligence—to praise a school for its triumphs on the playing field is not what most professors would call a compliment—but I wonder whether our traditional conceptions of intelligence have been too limited. We academics tend to stress the importance of abstract reasoning, and logic is certainly one of the glories of the human mind, but it's hardly the whole story. If the brain is not a unified monolith but a constellation of programs, each with its own aptitudes and liabilities, it follows that there are many sorts of intelligence, each representing excellence in one or more of the programs. We are not apt to understand human (much less extraterrestrial) intelligence until we begin to appreciate that it comes in many forms, and that all are valuable.

I got to thinking anew about athleticism and the brain during the 1989 professional football season, when I was teaching at Berkeley and following the San Francisco 49ers. It was a happy time: Brilliantly coached and enviably balanced, the 49ers that year ranked among the most sophisticated—and insouciant—football teams ever to take the field. As the sportswriter Robert Oates, Jr., put it, they "seemed to mock the machismo of its sport. Nothing looked hard. Everything looked easy. The 'Niners threw short, they threw long, they ran outside, they ran inside—and they did it all with a creative grace that spoke less of brute force than ballet." Watching them play, I began to recognize how much we have to learn about intelligence right here on Earth.

Several of the players on that extraordinary club I would call geniuses, by which I mean that they played so creatively that they innovated the sport.

One was Ronnie Lott, the free safety and as such the 49ers' last line of defense. Daunting as a Frankish ax-wielder in black gloves and a pair of black arm protectors that made him look as though he prepared for each game by dipping his forearms in boiling Butyl, Lott dominated the deep backfield like a creature imported from a slightly more massive planet. Physically gifted—he could run backward faster than most men can run forward, and cut sideways as abruptly as a light beam bounced off a mirror— Lott was equally impressive for the intellectual resourcefulness he brought to the game.

I remember one play in particular that exemplified Lott's imaginative approach to football. Early in San Francisco's pivotal 1989 playoff game against their old adversaries the Los Angeles Rams, Lott found himself on the far side of the field from Rams receiver Flipper Anderson, who had beaten his man and was loitering alone near the goal line, watching a pass from quarterback Jim Everett spiral toward him for what seemed a certain score. Moving with unmitigated confidence, Lott sped across the field, took to the air, and slapped the ball away perhaps a yard short of Anderson's outstretched hands. For Lott to have gotten to the ball in time was memorable as a physical accomplishment, but astonishing, too, was the audacity of imagination that had enabled him to *think* that he could get there—the vision that inspired him to go for the ball rather than the receiver, knowing that if he arrived a split second late Anderson would score a touchdown. The point was lost neither on Anderson (who left the field shaking his head and muttering, "He came out of nowhere") nor on the Rams, who were shut out for the rest of the afternoon and lost the game 30–3.

A genius on the offense was Jerry Rice, a wiry, buoyant wide receiver never more at ease than when in motion. Most receivers going downfield will fake, throwing a foot or a hip one way and cutting another, but Rice generally just ran. At full speed he looked as relaxed as a man in an easy chair, and it was his habit when a pass came his way to look back unhurriedly, as if hearing someone whisper his name, then gather in the spinning football with as little fuss as if he were opening his mail. What ensued might be a sprint to the goal line or the horrifying crash into the small of his back of an angry and frustrated defensive back, but in either case Rice customarily reacted with imperturbable good cheer. So renowned was his equanimous demeanor on the field that once, when he politely disagreed with two officials who had declared him out of bounds when catching a sideline pass, the referees actually turned to each other and began discussing his testimony—behavior as astounding as if police detectives were to consider releasing a suspect simply because he told them he was innocent. (A videotape replay showed that Rice was right, and the pass was ruled complete.)

But the player who particularly intrigued me, from a neurological point of view, was Joe Montana. To play quarterback in the National Football League calls for speed (the quarterback has on average two and a half seconds in which to take the snap from center, drop back, set, spot a receiver, and throw a pass; a handoff play may take less than one second), deception (while doing all this he tries to appear to be doing something else, lest the defense read his intentions), precision (if you can *consistently* chuck a football into a trash can buckled in the passenger seat of a swerving jeep twenty yards away, you may have what it takes), initiative (if the play as called doesn't work the quarterback tries to improvise), and poise (he must stay cool while a half dozen of the strongest and most violently aggressive men in the world pursue him with the cherished intention of slamming him to the ground so hard that he'll walk off the field, hang up his shoulder pads, and restrict his future athletic endeavors to golf).

Born to this singular calling, Montana by 1989 was ranked by many, among them the legendary quarterbacks Joe Namath, Bart Starr, Roger Staubach, and Terry Bradshaw, as the greatest quarterback ever. They were impressed not only by his statistics but by his sheer nonchalance. Montana executed nearly every play, even a final-second heartstopper in a championship game, with the lighthearted composure of a kid in a sandlot game who doesn't yet know what it is to lose. Physically lithe and fit but otherwise unexceptional-looking, Montana was bright, pleasant, and unprepossessing to the point of blandness: Asked at a postgame press conference following the 49ers' 55–10 rout of the Denver Broncos in the 1990 Super Bowl what he planned to do next, he replied, "I'm going to take a nice nap."

What was Montana's secret? To be a genius is to *have* genius, somewhere among the centers of the brain. The genius of a great musician might reside in the right frontal lobe, a poet's in the left lobe. I think the locus of Joe Montana's genius was to be found in his premotor cortex.

The impulse to carry out actions is conveyed through the nervous system to the muscles from the brain's motor cortex, a belt of gray tissue that arches across the forebrain and terminates just in front of each ear. When we walk or run—or hand off a football to a running back—it is the impulses conveyed by neurons in motor cortex that incite the striated muscles in our feet, legs, arms, and hands to act. The motor cortex, in turn, selects specific actions from what amounts to a dictionary stored in the supplementary motor area, located at the top of the brain. Together these two centers are capable of handling individual actions, but not complex sequences: Using motor cortex and supplementary motor area alone a quarterback might be able to take a snap from center or throw a pass, but he would be unable to do these things in rapid succession. To coordinate a sequence of actions he must call on the *pre*motor cortex, a strip of brain tissue located immediately in front of the motor cortex.

It is by virtue of instructions programmed into premotor cortex that an athlete can blend together a series of acts much more rapidly and smoothly than would be the case if the brain had to invent each motion in real time. We see the premotor cortex ablaze in all its glory when we listen to the seemingly effortless playing of the cellist Yo-Yo Ma, or watch the dancing of the late Fred Astaire. Joe Montana, whom Joe Namath aptly described as "football's Fred Astaire," was smoothness incarnate. "With most guys, it's, 'I see. I step. I throw,'" said John Madden, the sports commentator and former coach of the Oakland Raiders. "With Montana, it's, 'I seestepthrow.'"

The programs in Montana's premotor cortex were distinguished not only by their seamless weave but by their duration, by the length of the chain. Montana could check off two covered receivers and throw to a third man, sometimes even finding a way to get the ball to a covered receiver, in part because he didn't have to reflect on the situation at the time. Most of what he had to do was already programmed into his premotor cortex; to introduce conscious decision-making into the process would usually wreck his timing. As Montana remarked, "If I ever stopped to think about what happens, what really makes things tick, after the ball hits my hands, it might screw up the whole process."

The importance of premotor cortex to professional athletes helps us understand their penchant for practicing hard. Watching Montana and Rice work out one sunny afternoon at their training camp in Santa Clara, I was struck by the fact that they moved just as fast in practice as when playing a game. Dressed in sweat suits and deprived of their shoulder pads and jerseys, they looked like an ordinary bunch of guys playing touch ball at a Sunday picnic—until the ball was snapped, whereupon all was transformed into a blur of amazing grace. Obedient to a dictum introduced by Rice and running back Roger Craig, every ball carrier ran every play all the way to the end zone, the idea being to so condition their minds that scoring a touchdown would become, to borrow from computer lingo, their default position. The reason for practicing so assiduously was not physical; few top players nowadays rely on practice sessions for conditioning. Nor did it have much to do with acquiring new knowledge; Montana and Rice were not *learning* how to handle the ball. Rather, they were doing what violinists and pianists do when they practice—tuning up their premotor cortex—and this works best when done in earnest. To hold back in practice would be to load an inferior program, one that might later surface as poor play in a real game. Better always to do it right, in the spirit of the harpsichordist Wanda Landowska, who said, "I never practice; I always play." To practice hard is to load the right program. "As the ball is snapped I picture the play," Montana noted in his autobiography. "It's like a movie running through my mind."

This in turn sheds light on athletes' emphasis on attitude. The importance of maintaining a winning attitude is sometimes put in mystical terms, as if it were a secret that only initiates could understand, but it becomes less mysterious if we view it as a way of keeping the conscious mind from interfering with the functioning of premotor programs geared to success. Ronnie Lott often counseled his teammates before a game to visualize how they wanted to play, then keep that vision firmly in mind until the game was over. Don't watch the *other* team play, he would say; keep your mind on *your* performance. "You've got to mentally dominate the game," said Harry Edwards, a sociology professor at Berkeley and a former athlete who served on the 49ers' coaching staff. "I've never known a great athlete who did not have as his basic attitude, not *if* he was going to win, but *how* he was going to win."

Which may explain why good teams so often play their worst games against bad teams. Competition (from the Latin *con petire*, "to seek together") is a two-way street, and the best-laid plans of premotor cortex can go awry when executed against an opponent who errs. The great running back O. J. Simpson used to rehearse patterns constantly in his mind; when driving in traffic he would pretend that the other cars were defensive players, and think about how to run through them. So long as his opponents did what they were supposed to do, Simpson's careful planning helped produce the kind of results that earned him a career total of 11,236 yards gained, one of the highest in football history; but Simpson was vulnerable to tackle by defensive backs who botched their assignments and found themselves in his path accidentally. The 49ers were like that. The only decisive loss they posted in the 1989 season was to the inconsequential Green Bay Packers, who played so inconsistently that they confused the 'Niners, beating them 21–17.

As one might expect from a premotor cortex virtuoso, Montana relied especially heavily on attitude. "For a quarterback the game is at least seventy per cent mental," he said. His performance could plummet alarmingly if a few plays went wrong and he began to lose confidence in the movie in his head, but he tended to recover quickly on the sidelines, seldom permitting a poor series of downs to interfere with his global vision of ultimate victory.* Outright defeats he regarded with Olympian indifference, as corruptions of the Platonic ideal; accosted by a fan after botching a last-minute drive in a playoff game the 49ers should have won, he replied breezily, "Haven't you ever had a bad day at the office?"

Individuals begin to look a bit different once one starts thinking of each as a galaxy of intelligences, and I would go so far as to conjecture that you could read signs of Montana's physical excellence in his relatively expressionless face. Joe smiled a lot, on the field and off,

---

*When things went well, Montana kept his edge by setting himself new challenges. Early in the fourth quarter of San Francisco's 1990 Super Bowl win, Montana, rather than basking in the glory, sidled up to head coach George Seifert on the sidelines and suggested that the team should start thinking about winning a third straight Super Bowl the following season. (The 'Niners came within one game of that goal, but were beaten by the New York Giants in the National Conference championship game after Montana was sidelined with a broken finger.)

but his was a static smile of repose, rather like a dolphin's. This inexpressive countenance strikes a familiar chord: It is the embodiment of "cool"—the mask worn by Buster Keaton, the most accomplished athlete among the silent screen stars, and by Steve McQueen, who in the film *Bullitt* permits himself only the slightest knit of the brow when a gangster he is pursuing at the climax of a high-speed car chase blows out the windshield of his Mustang with a shotgun.

I suspect that the genesis of this mask can be traced to developments in cortical tissue produced by sustained athletic training. Control over the various parts of the body is localized in specific cortical regions, and these regions can be mapped. (It is from such studies that researchers derived the homunculus diagrams that one sees in textbooks, where arraigned along the cortical strip are large areas for controlling the hands and face, and smaller ones for the knees, trunk, and shoulders.) For years it was assumed that the relative sizes of each cortical zone were more or less fixed throughout an adult's life, but in the 1980s researchers learned that in sensory cortex, at least, the size of a given region increases when the part of the body to which it corresponds is used more often. When, for instance, a monkey whose cortical map was being monitored was trained to hold a finger against a vibrating surface, the number of cortical cells devoted to processing sensations coming from that fingertip increased on a daily basis. Presumably the same is true of humans, so that when a child learns to play the piano or an adult practices card tricks, the area of somatosensory cortex devoted to the fingers grows in size. It seems reasonable to propose that this phenomenon occurs in motor cortex as well, so that a map of a belly dancer's motor cortex would show proportionately more cells devoted to controlling the abdominal muscles, and a hurdler's more cells devoted to the legs and feet.

Growth in one region of cortex comes at the expense of adjacent regions. And what lies next, on the cortex, to the hand? The face. Assign more cortex to control of the hands, and you are borrowing from brain tissue that otherwise would be devoted to the face. We would expect, say, that an actor who constantly practiced facial expressions would enlarge the cortical area that operates her face—and that, conversely, a quarterback's cortical map would prove to have relatively more area devoted to his hands and wrists. Motor cortex is bifurcated, with facial and related muscles assigned to half of a normal individual's cortical tissue while the other half handles hands, arms, trunk, legs, and so forth; possibly the frontier between the two realms migrates in response to disproportionate demands for control of a given realm.

So it just may be that the cool, almost expressionless face of an athlete like Joe Montana is the outward badge of a motor cortex so skilled at managing the hands and feet that it has depleted the cortical territory normally employed to control facial muscles. We respond to the mask precisely because we have learned to associate it with competence in action. That's why macho movie stars like Clint Eastwood and Arnold Schwarzenegger underact like crazy. The critics may complain that their unvarying facial expressions get tiresome after a while, but Eastwood and Schwarzenegger know what they are doing: They are playing men whose intelligence lies in deeds, not talk, and whose motor cortex, consequently, has borrowed tissue from mere expression in order to devote it to large-muscle functions like running, jumping, and firing endless clips of ammunition from automatic weapons.

But isn't all this merely a roundabout way of saying that athletes are just dumb jocks after all—that they have sacrificed their "higher" brains on the altar of athletic excellence?

I don't think so, and I'll tell you why. Motor and premotor cortex are *part* of the higher brain, and can claim credit for some of our loftiest achievements. Anatomically, both are closely related to the brain centers responsible for language: Broca's area, the section of the brain that processes speech, belongs to the premotor cortex. This association between talking and acting leads some brain researchers to hypothesize that our ability to speak and write—one of the hallmarks of intellectuality—evolved as a byproduct of selection for advanced athletic skills, in particular the ability to bring down wild animals by throwing stones and spears. The American neurobiologist William H. Calvin suggests that "the supposed specialization of the left brain for language is probably just a secondary effect of a more primitive specialization of the left hemisphere for handling sequences." If Calvin is correct, the cortical development that graces our species with its unique ability to speak and to write was driven less by intellectual challenges than by advances in human athletic competence.* This is not surprising, if you consider that speaking is itself an intricate physical feat: From the point of view of the premotor cortex, articulating long strings of syllables is a lot like climbing a rock face or pitching a baseball game. In performance, Kenneth Branagh the Shakespearean actor and Joe Montana the quarterback are exercising many of the same areas of their brains.

Very well, one might argue, perhaps language was made possible by physical prowess, and if so we are no more justified in deriding an inarticulate athlete than in making

*We see this evolutionary sequence recapitulated in the development of children, who ordinarily cannot begin talking until they learn to walk. Walking like talking is a complex task, and the left-hemisphere motor cortex normally responsible for coordinating both functions must reach a certain stage of development before the child can manage either. "Talk before you go / Your tongue will be your overthrow," says a Victorian bromide.

fun of an orator who can't play tennis. But what of logic? Surely here, in the realm of abstract thought, the higher brain soars far above its sweaty origins in ball-playing and spear-throwing. Are not intellectuals justified in regarding the pure thinking of Einstein and Euler as superior to the merely physical feats of Michael Jordan or Martina Navratilova?

Not really, for the abstract thinking of scientists is a great deal more physical than is usually assumed. The great theoretical physicists, however much their completed theories may be couched in the ethereality of mathematical equations, usually think in terms of mental models, which are but substitutes for physical constructions built of balsa wood, sealing wax, and string. "I never satisfy myself until I can make a mechanical model of a thing," said Lord Kelvin, the giant of classical thermodynamics. "If I can make a mechanical model I can understand it. As long as I cannot make a mechanical model all the way through I cannot understand." Einstein's "thought experiments," though they led him to counterintuitive conceptions like particulate light and plastic time, were based on information garnered from real experiments. Much the same was true of Archimedes and Galileo, whose investigations of physics owed a lot to their scrutiny of ropes and levers at work in boatyards and docks, and of Newton, who said that "the proper method of inquiring after the properties of things is to deduce them from experiments." The grand abstractions of science work not because they are abstract, but because they are firmly anchored in the gritty reality of the physical world. And while it is true that *pure* mathematics can get pretty abstruse, it too sprang from the interrogation of the tangible: Number theory began with counting, and geometry, for Plato the very emblem of pure thought, originated with the efforts of

Egyptian "rope stretchers" to survey property lines in oft-flooded farmlands adjoining the Nile.

My point, in any case, is not that quantum mechanics or the mathematics of Cantor sets are *less* miraculous than the spectacle of Ronnie Lott knocking away that pass in the 'Niners-Rams game—not, to put it another way, that a great scientist is less to be esteemed than a great athlete—but that they are equally to be esteemed. The higher brain centers that create poems and symphonies and theories of chemical bonding are not "better" than the centers responsible for mere running and jumping and play; as the American physicist Richard Feynman liked to say, "Nothing is 'mere.'" If those of us who contemplate the prospect of extraterrestrial life were to spend more time trying to grasp the diversity of intelligence here on Earth, we might be less quick to fix on one-dimensional paradigms that rank panstellar brainpower in terms of smart and dumb, and in doing so become a little less dumb ourselves.

If you're still unconvinced that it takes just as much brainpower (albeit of a somewhat different kind) to play center field for the Red Sox as to teach anthropology at Harvard, consider what has been going on in the "artificial intelligence" field. There scientists are finding, to their surprise, that it is harder for a computer to coordinate sequences of physical actions than to solve abstract problems.

Modern computers are pretty good at carrying out logical tasks of the sort that their programmers tend to value as intelligent. They can solve in seconds equations in higher mathematics that would consume a human's efforts for years. (Indeed, we are beginning to see mathematical proofs that *only* a computer can solve; they make mathematicians uneasy, but nobody except another computer has the time and the dogged devotion to check up on whether the computer was right.) They can also play a wicked game of chess; by the early 1990s only the world chess champion and a few of his peers could beat top computer programs like Deep Thought, which while pondering its next move examines up to 450,000 positions a second.

What computers can't do very well is to *act*. The simplest physical tasks are hard for them. At the Goddard Space Flight Center, NASA's leading center for robotics, a robot arm programmed to open a door in a laboratory demonstration instead ripped the door off its hinges. (The computer needed a better feedback loop, like the one that communicates between Joe Montana's motor cortex and his right arm.) Another robot, programmed to lock down a mock space station component, reached tentatively toward the part and then froze; somebody had turned on an overhead light, and the robot's sensors could not adjust to the difference in lighting. Engineers at NASA's Jet Propulsion Laboratory tried for years to build a computer-controlled "rover," the prototype for an automated vehicle that would roam the surface of Mars; though equipped with video cameras, a laser rangefinder, and a state-of-the-art high-speed computer, the rover never did manage to find its way around the lab parking lot.

The problem, in the view of Hans Moravec, director of the Mobile Robot Laboratory at Carnegie Mellon University, is that robotics researchers "set their sights directly on the intellectual acme of human thought, in experiments running on large, stationary mainframe computers dedicated to mechanizing pure reasoning." But physical acuity is *not* an inferior version of logical thought; it is a separate and equal realm of intelligence that must be mastered on its own terms.

Those terms are largely unconscious and ineffable, which is why we usually do better at carrying out a sequence of

actions—parallel parking a car, say, or throwing a baseball—
if we don't think overmuch about what we are doing. A
student quoted in Eugen Herrigel's *Zen in the Art of Archery*
asks the master,

> "How can the shot be loosed if 'I' do not do it?"
> " 'It' shoots," he replied.
> . . . "And who or what is this 'It'?"
> "Once you have understood that," the master replied, "you
> will have no further need of me."

Mastery of that ineffable "it" is what athletes demonstrate
every day, and what computers are nowhere near accom-
plishing.

Historically, the physical was the inventor of the
intellectual—we spent millions of years evolving the wisdom
of the body, as against perhaps one hundred thousand
years for rational thought—and children are forever reen-
acting this old drama. The learning child *acts;* he reaches
for blocks, experiments with stacking them (there is no
"wrong" way to do this), then transforms the stack, through
the magic of the imagination, into a castle or a fort. The
child who simply stares into space is probably not thinking
abstract thoughts; he is probably not doing very well at all.

The profundity of the body's wisdom is highlighted in the
talents of the abnormal—among great athletes, at one
extreme, and, at another, among the brain-damaged in-
mates of mental wards. One of the great tragedies in the
recent history of mental health institutions, much remarked
upon by researchers, has been our blindness to the extraordinary abilities of autistic children and idiot savants. These
are people whose speech centers have been damaged,
leaving them cut off from their companions, but whose
physical intelligence is often highly developed. Because

they cannot talk normally, they have too often been classified as morons. Typically, they display a great interest in machinery. The psychologist Bernard Rimland describes one of his patients, an autistic youth named Joe:

> He recently put together a tape recorder, fluorescent light and a small transistor radio with some other components so that music from the tape was changed to light energy in the light and then back to music in the radio. By passing his hand between the recorder and the light, he could stop the music. He understands the concepts of electronics, astronomy, music, navigation, and mechanics. He knows how things work and is familiar with technical terms. By the age of 12 he could find his way all over the city on his bike with a map and compass. He reads Bowditch on navigation. He is supposed to have an IQ of 80. He does assembly work in a Goodwill store.

This Joe, I suspect, is fascinated by machinery because the most highly developed part of his brain is the part concerned with the mechanical manipulation of objects. In this he shows signs of genius, as Joe Montana is a genius at throwing a football. Viewed with the eye of our understanding, both Joes remind us that we need not look solely to the stars in order to behold a wealth of wildly differing varieties of intelligence. Each human mind is a galaxy of intelligences, wherein shines the light of a billion stars.

Belly Laughs

Progress is nothing but the victory of laughter over dogma.

—Benjamin DeCasseres

Comedy is a serious business.

—Buster Keaton

I began thinking about laughter as a window on the brain one night when my four-year-old son—having wheedled his way into bed with my wife and me in the middle of the night and promptly fallen back to sleep, leaving me wide awake in the dark—suddenly laughed in his sleep. It was a lovely sound, a deep, heartfelt chuckle that bubbled into a belly laugh that was remarkably sonorous, considering that it came from so small a belly. I wondered what had made him laugh. That started me wondering what makes *anybody* laugh.

A difficult question. Laughter is found in every human culture, yet every community sports at least one sourpuss. It is notoriously difficult to predict just what will make people laugh—producers of comedy films know all too well that a scene that draws guffaws from one audience may meet with stony silence from another audience, two hours later, in the same theater. Yet some humor is accepted universally; Charlie Chaplin is as popular today in China as in the

United States. We laugh at a joke, which is a cerebral stimulus, and also at being tickled, which is physical, but while the laughs sound the same they are subtly different: I can for instance crack myself up by saying something funny, but I cannot make myself laugh by tickling myself. Every laugh is a paradox.

Eventually I left off trying to sleep, got up and went to my study, and began paging through the books of the great thinkers to read their ideas about the nature of laughter. I was still at it months later.

There are, I learned, some eighty distinct theories of why people laugh, and they concur on almost nothing. Some authors maintain that a sense of humor is inborn, others that it is acquired. Most see humor as a universal human attribute, but a few, emphasizing the painful truth that some people simply have no sense of humor, argue that laughter is a skill that must be mastered, like riding a bicycle. Many assume that it is fun to laugh, but Henri Bergson in his celebrated essay on humor maintains that laughter is devoid of emotion: "Indifference is its natural environment, for laughter has no greater foe than emotion," Bergson writes. ". . . Its appeal is to intelligence, pure and simple." I had imagined that my little boy laughed because he'd seen something funny in a dream, but Sigmund Freud informed me that the human child "lacks all feeling for the comic." Hegel regarded humor as essentially aggressive, while Chaplin and Walt Disney saw nothing particularly hostile about a good laugh. (On this last point we may be seeing the difference between an artist and a critic; Disney and Chaplin were funny, while I doubt that Hegel could have provoked a laugh to save his life.)

The experts, I found, differ even on so fundamental a question as whether it is a good thing to have a sense of humor. Certainly laughter is "the best medicine," as the jokes column in *Reader's Digest* had it—the journalist Norman Cousins engineered his recovery from a potentially fatal illness through a regimen that included repeated viewing of Marx Brothers comedies, a feat that helped earn him a faculty post at the UCLA Medical School—but whatever its physical benefits, laughter is regarded in some circles as *infra dig*. Ecclesiastes declares that "a fool lifteth up his voice with laughter, but a wise man doth scarce smile a little." Lord Chesterfield advised his famously over-counseled son that "loud laughter is the mirth of the mob, who are only pleased with silly things; for true wit or good sense never excited a laugh since the creation of the world. A man of parts and fashion is therefore only seen to smile, but never heard to laugh." I even came across one dour expert who dismissed the love of humor as idiosyncratic to the Saxon peoples; that hypothesis got a good laugh from a Samoan friend of mine.

What we have, then, is a mystery within the human brain as deep as anything we've found among the stars. Why is it that laughter poses such a paradox, so that the philosophers and psychologists have found it necessary to invent such outlandishly serious and mutually exclusive arguments to account for it?

Having pondered this question at length, I think I have the answer—one that sheds light on the nature of the brain and, therefore, on the role of the mind in a cosmic context. Like the philosophers who have preceded me I feel confident that my theory of laughter alone is correct, and will banish all others as surely as the rising sun evaporates the dew. Like them, I will explain my theory with unwavering seriousness, thus ensuring that while it may not seem funny today, it is certain to draw laughs in the future. (As Cervantes remarked, "It is difficult not to write satire.")

The essence of my theory is that laughter arises from the

interaction of two important programs in the human brain, one of which constructs plausible models of reality while the other challenges such models. (In reality there probably are more than two programs involved, but for simplicity's sake I will treat them as only two, in something like the way that historians treat two great armies as individuals although each contains many corps.) If I am correct, laughter presents us with conspicuous evidence of the multipartite brain at work, and the difficulties that have beset previous efforts to understand laughter have arisen from the mistaken assumption that the brain is best regarded as singular.

This is what I think is happening:

The mind is confronted every day with the task of making sense of the universe, and of one's self, and of one's place in the universe. To do this it has evolved a model-building program. This program is sober, responsible, creative, and assured—the domain, if you like, of the god Apollo. The Apollo program (as I will call it, with apologies to NASA) works across a wide spectrum of time and space, rendering sensory data into perceived objects from moment to moment, while on larger and longer scales producing our conceptions of our fellow human beings and our world.

The Apollo program, however, works imperfectly. All the models it creates are flawed in one way or another—they are, after all, only models—and if they went unchallenged we would spend most of our time immersed in delusion. (Perhaps we do anyway, but that's another subject.) Delusion can be dangerous: The tree dweller who grabs a rotten branch under the misapprehension that it is a sound branch is in trouble; so is a camper who mistakes fetid water for good water, or a pearl diver who thinks a stonefish is a stone. Therefore the brain has evolved a second program, responsible for challenging the models that the Apollo program builds. *This* program is irreverent, skeptical, and playful—the domain of Pan.

All comedy puts these two gods on display. The banker is Apollo; W. C. Fields as the Bank Dick is Pan. The commencement speaker is Apollo; the streaker who interrupts his lofty pronouncements is Pan. Society needs both. It is pointless to deride a pompous professor for being a stick-in-the-mud, or to complain that a comedian lacks respect for our cherished institutions; both are simply doing their jobs, by embodying, respectively, the god that builds and maintains models and the god that mocks them and tears them down. (The tragedy of scientific creativity is that the great scientist begins as Pan, coming up with new theories that supplant the old, and then in defending them is transformed into Apollo; that, I think, is why few theoretical physicists do creative work much past the age of forty.)

When the Pan program discovers a dangerous fault in a model constructed by the Apollo program the situation is not funny—at least not to the person threatened by the discrepancy. Imagine that you are strolling down a path in the jungle. Thanks to the Apollo program, you see "objects" all around—trees, vines, a bird in flight, a stick on the ground in the path. Thanks to the Pan program, these models are constantly being interrogated. When the Pan program spots a threatening discrepancy between reality and representation—that "stick" is not a stick but a venomous snake, a fer-de-lance, camouflaged against the leaf litter on the trail!—it activates mechanisms that prepare brain and body to deal with the threat. If the danger is perceived as immediate and severe, the limbic system produces a cascade of chemicals (principally corticotropin releasing hormone, which in turn triggers the release into the bloodstream of adrenocorticotropic hormone and cortisol) that result in a sudden increase in brain alertness and body tension, producing a state known generically as "stress." These chemicals prime the body to perform with unusual speed and strength: Time slows down, perceptions are heightened, and muscle power increases dramatically.

But when the danger proves to be groundless—if the snake turns out to be a stick after all—you are left with the alarm bells ringing to no purpose: The fight-or-flee chemicals are surging through the bloodstream, all dressed up and nowhere to go. Vigorous physical exercise can help dispel stress; so can meditation. But the quickest and easiest way to discharge stress is by emitting a convulsive bark, a paroxysm of brain and body, what one authority described as "spasmodic contractions of the large and small zygomatic (facial) muscles and sudden relaxations of the diaphragm accompanied by contractions of the laryns and epiglottis"— in short, by laughing.

A laugh, then, results when the Pan program spots a potentially dangerous error in a model crafted by the Apollo program but the error turns out to be harmless, so that stress is first aroused and then quickly dispelled.

The greater the amount of stress, the more likely we are to laugh once it is relieved. This can happen without anything being particularly funny. Charles Darwin cited the example of soldiers "who after strong excitement from exposure to extreme danger were particularly apt to burst into loud laughter at the smallest joke." When I was an editor at *Rolling Stone* magazine an armed band of Hell's Angels stormed into my office one afternoon and threatened to dangle me by my ankles out the window, from which vantage point I could contemplate the sidewalk five stories below. (They were angry about an article that had appeared in the magazine.) So long as they contented themselves with conversation instead of defenestration I can assure you that I felt quite merry indeed.

Low comedy works on this level, dispelling stress simply by redirecting it outward. We laugh at the pratfalls of clowns because we are all a bit anxious about hurting ourselves—especially by falling, the bane of our tree-dwelling ancestors—and so feel relieved to see that someone can act even more awkwardly than we do yet survive the fall. Humor of this sort can easily turn cruel—as when children laugh at the sight of an ordinary mortal slipping on a banana peel, not realizing that he *can* be hurt—but it is a mistake to conclude, as Hegel did, that *all* comedy is cruel. Low comedy is only one form of the comic; it relieves our tensions but teaches us little, and as such it is disdained by those who can do better. ("Life is too serious to do farce comedy," said Buster Keaton, who after performing an exquisite bit of custard pie throwing for a 1939 Hollywood retrospective on the silent film era mused glumly that never before in his long career had he found it necessary to throw a pie.)

High comedy adds another ingredient; it not only relieves stress, but discloses an imperfection in the model of reality that *produced* the stress. In doing so it teaches us something. The laugh discharges our anxiety while we delight in having learned something new.

That is why the best jokes are about serious subjects like sex, inadequacy, death, and taxes. Charlie Chaplin believed that the underlying theme of his tramp character was mortality: "I am always aware that Charlie is playing with death," he said. "He plays with it, mocks it, thumbs his nose at it, but it is always there. He is aware of death at every moment of his existence, and he is terribly aware of being alive." When Lenny Bruce on his opening night at the Blue Angel in New York City borrowed Wilt Chamberlin's cigarette, examined the filter tip, then said, with an air of astonishment, "He *niggerlipped* it!" he got a laugh because there was quite enough racism in the atmosphere to make the insult authentically shocking, and its evaporation into a joke legitimately enlightening. (Because he maintained that hurtful words lose their sting once we laugh at them, Bruce made enemies among those who confuse words with reality.)

The dependency of laughter on stress imposes upon humor a kind of law of conservation of energy. A comic can get a quick laugh by eliciting relatively little stress and promptly dispelling it, even though the punchline reveals but a trivial insight. If she takes longer to build a joke, raising the level of stress, the punchline must be worthier or else the joke will collapse under its own weight. Most professional comedians exploit this law by working fast; the average standup comic gets off a punchline every ten or fifteen seconds. When Henny Youngman says, "I found a solution to the parking problem—I bought a parked car," he may not have revealed anything very profound, but we laugh because the anxiety we had to undergo to get to the payoff—a moment's attention to the parking problem —did not represent much of an investment.

Economy, not brevity, is the soul of wit. A master comedian can afford to work slowly, building the tension higher, provided that he has more to reveal at the punchline. Jack Benny on a 1957 episode of his television series pulled off a joke that consumed nearly ten full minutes of air time. The premise is that the head of a Hollywood studio wants to talk with Benny about making a film of his life story. Benny, whose last movie, *The Horn Blows at Midnight*, was a flop, is elevated to delusions of grandeur by his anticipated return to movie stardom. When he and his wife arrive and are let through the gate by a security guard, Benny orders his driver, Rochester, to park in the spot reserved for the president of the studio. No sooner has Rochester brought the car to a halt than a gunshot rings out. The three look up in astonishment to see that the security guard has fired a bullet through the radiator of Benny's car.

"What's the big idea of shooting at us?" Benny demands of Herman, the guard.

"You took the space reserved for Mr. Adler," Herman replies.

"Oh," says Benny. "I'm terribly sorry. . . . You see, I'm Jack Benny and I've got an appointment with . . ."

"Jack Benny?"

"Yes."

"The one that starred in *The Horn Blows at Midnight*?"

"Yes, yes. I made that for Warner Brothers years ago. Did you see it?"

"See it?" the guard replies. "I *directed* it."

That's a marvelous punchline, but note that to build the gag over so long a period, Benny and his writers had to push the tension and incongruity of the situation to almost unbelievable levels. This was true of many of Benny's jokes, some of which moved so slowly that they devolved into silence. In his most famous gag, confronted by a mugger who growls, "Your money or your life!" Benny said nothing; by the time he finally delivered the punchline—"I'm *thinking it over!*"—he had drawn what has been described as the longest laugh in radio history.

The most profound jokes invoke paradox, the ultimate incongruity. Their subject is the inadequacy, not just of a particular model of reality, but of *all* models. They attack the very basis of the Apollo program, reminding us that no paradigm fully reflects reality. Their target is every individual who imagines that his is the one correct view of life.

That, I suppose, is why there is a robust tradition of paradox in the humor of Jews, who have suffered so frequently at the hands of true believers. Freud quotes a joke about an old Jew who tries to play cards with a friend but gives up in frustration at the other man's clumsiness and ignorance of the game: Throwing down his cards in disgust, he says, "What can I expect from a man who plays cards with *me?*"

"I wouldn't belong to any club that would have me for a member," said Groucho Marx, resurrecting the same joke (and improving it; Groucho was a great lapidarist). Groucho's joke strikes not just at antisemitism but at all systems of rigid thought and belief. They all have knots, you see, where the ruled parallel lines of faith and logic snake together and spiral away like water down a drain. Most of us ignore the knots most of the time, and act as if our assumptions about life and the universe were as true as planed hardwood. Gadflies like Einstein and Bohr and Keaton and Marx gather at the knots, and drill there, and sometimes break through to glimpse another way of looking at the world. The new system may be better or worse, but it, too, will be inadequate. The gadflies know this, but go on drilling anyway. That is their job—to punch holes in belief systems and let the light shine through, awakening the rest of us.

The imperative that wit involves wisdom holds true even (or perhaps especially) when the humor is unintentional. Years ago, as a boy growing up in south Florida, I heard an Army general stationed at Cape Canaveral being interviewed on a radio program. He was asked why he did not think it advisable to arc missiles carrying polar-orbit satellites directly over Miami, though this would have been more efficient than routing them out to sea. "Should a missile crash into downtown Miami," the general replied thoughtfully, "the result could be massive loss of life and destruction of property, and that would be harmful to the morale of my men." What made this remark funny, it seems to me, is that the general revealed himself to be doing exactly what he ought to be doing—concerning himself above all else with the welfare of the soldiers under his command—even though the incongruity of his outlook, in ranking their morale above the specter of a rocket-fuel fireball engulfing downtown Miami, was enough to make a civilian's jaw drop.

Unquestionably, humor can be a fearsome weapon. Comedians recounting a triumphant show say, "I *destroyed* them; I *killed* them; I *murdered* them." The Germans have a word for it—*auslachen,* which means to attack and disarm someone by making jokes at his expense. Among African and Arctic peoples there are some who practice formal duels of wit, in which two conflicting males, rather than fighting, take turns insulting each other until one is judged to have triumphed by uttering a conclusive *bon mot,* whereupon the two adversaries shake hands and bury the hatchet. (A similar institution can be found in African-American communities, where it is known variously as "mother ranking" and "doing the dozens.")

Physical violence, too, abounds in comedy. The young Chaplin, said his friend the juggler Blaise Cendrars, "had a way of kicking people which was wonderful to behold." W. C. Fields' most popular act, the famous bent-pool-cue routine, ended with his pretending to brain his partner with the cue; on one occasion, when Fields discovered that his partner was drawing laughs by mugging the audience while crouched beneath the pool table, Fields dispensed with pretense and knocked the man unconscious. Buster Keaton as a child performed a routine in which he was regularly beaten black and blue by his father, a heavy drinker. If Keaton flinched, his father would hiss at him, "Face! Face!" "That meant freeze the puss," Keaton recalled.

    . . . . In this knockabout act, my father and I used to hit each other with brooms, occasioning for me strange flops and falls. If I should chance to smile, the next hit would be

a good deal harder. All the parental correction I ever
received was with an audience looking on. I could not even
whimper.

But violence is a catalyst of wit, not its final product. A
joke that arouses anger but then dispels it is very different
from a cruel joke that leaves the anger unassuaged; as
Cervantes said, "Jests which slap the face are not good jests."
A really good joke creates tension not merely to dispel it,
but to reveal something to us as well. As Kant remarked,
"Laughter is an affection arising from the sudden transfor-
mation of a strained expectation into nothing." The expectation must be strained, or we would not be close enough to
seeing through the paradigm to get the joke. The paradigm
is transformed into nothing in the sense that it is exposed for
what it is, a thin and tattered tissue hung between our tender
sensibilities and the cold reality of an uncaring universe.

The chemistry of stress and revelation makes it possible
for a profound insight to produce a laugh even if it's not at
all funny. I have often laughed out loud at first hearing a
composer's masterful turn of phrase in a symphony, or
watching a superlative gymnast perform on the parallel
bars, not because I found them incongruous but because I
hadn't previously imagined that such a thing could be done;
the deed called attention to a ludicrous disparity between
the splendor of the human performance and the poverty of
my preconceptions about its limits. (Freud became interested in the psychology of wit after his friend and pupil
Theodor Reik noticed that Freud's students responded with
a delighted laugh when the meaning of a dream was
revealed to them.) This phenomenon is the mirror image of
low comedy, in which the level of stress is high and that of
insight low. Here stress is at a minimum, insight at a
maximum. A great joke can cover the whole spectrum:

Harold Lloyd dangling from the hands of a clock high above a city street can be laughed at anywhere from the low comedy perspective that he's in danger to the high comedy perspective that he, like the rest of us, is a prisoner of time, and is doomed to die anyway.

Bergson to the contrary, the incongruity that sparks a laugh need not be purely intellectual. It can be mostly emotional. We laugh at dirty jokes because sex is a profoundly troubling subject, even if we learn nothing from the jokes except that we have company in our incomprehension. But we also disparage dirty jokes, as we do puns, because their intellectual content is usually so meager. The most rewarding jokes, again, are the most enlightening.

We take pleasure in laughter, then, both because we enjoy the release of the anxiety it provides, and (if the joke rises to any higher than a purely emotional level) because the brain delights in discovering incongruities between perception and reality. Schopenhauer came close to what I am trying to say when he identified humor as arising from the perceived distinction between abstract rational knowledge and the raw material of perception. The cause of laughter, he wrote, "is simply the sudden perception of the incongruity between a concept and the real objects which have been thought through it in some relation, and laughter itself is just the expression of this incongruity"—the incongruity, that is to say, between the "abstract and the concrete object of perception." ("Everything is contained in Schopenhauer," Chaplin told Blaise Cendrars, when he was a young man in London and contemplating a career in medicine.)

It follows that a genuinely serious man is more likely to display a healthy sense of humor than is a superficial man, since he is accustomed to constantly testing his version of reality against the facts, and must—*because* he is serious—learn to roll with the intellectual pratfalls that result when his models fail the test. "The more a man is capable of entire seriousness, the more heartily can he laugh," writes Schopenhauer. A sense of humor, as George Santayana remarked, is a sense of proportion, and to one who has a sense of *cosmic* proportion *every* human pretension is ridiculous. "In humor the little is made great and the great little, in order to destroy both, because all is equal in contrast with the infinite," wrote Samuel Coleridge, borrowing an idea from Jean Paul Richter.

Humor like anything else can be counterfeited, and there are always a few comics (Don Rickles comes to mind) who make a living less by being funny than by acting *as if* they were funny. The distinction lies in the genuine comedian's ability to relax the mainspring of anxiety by unveiling an insight. The insight bursts forth like a bull from behind the matador's cape. In tragedy the bull dies. In comedy he turns out to be Ferdinand.

Good jokes are enlightened, bad jokes unenlightened; that they resemble each other is just another example of nature's passion for camouflage. The fact that two patterns of behavior can look identical and yet arise from disparate casts of mind is emphasized in Zen Buddhism, the philosophy of Groucho Marx and Fuke.* Superficially, a Zen master sweeping the floor is doing exactly what an untutored monk is doing when *he* sweeps the floor, but in actuality, they are having two quite different experiences. The Zen master Bokushu made this point in a talk to the assembled monks: "If you are not yet clear about the Great Matter," he said, "it is like the funeral of one's parents; if you are already clear about it, it is like the funeral of one's parents."

---

*Fuke was a Zen master, dates unknown, renowned for his wicked sense of humor. His last words are the most generous—i.e., instructive—I have heard of. When Fuke lay dying, surrounded by friends, he thrust out his hand, palm up, and said, "Give me some money!"

Among all systems of thought, it is Zen that best isolates the universal human dilemma in which humor takes root. If I could adequately put the message of Zen in words (which I cannot) I would say that it affirms the fact that the mind strives to make sense of the human condition, while knowing that it does so in vain. The Zen master accepts the absurdity of life, then transcends it, by living life exactly as if it were worth living: He sleeps and eats and sweeps the floor, understanding the pointlessness of it all and yet doing it anyway. His life is devoid of intentional cruelty, panic, bathos, piety, preachiness, apology and explanation. These manifestations of illusion are replaced by an appreciation of the beauty and value of life as experience, so that he really can live each day as if it were his last.

The nearest I have approached to the flavor of enlightenment came one summer afternoon when I was seventeen years old. My father and I were working in a garden under the hot Florida sun, and he sent me to fetch three rakes. I returned with the rakes, but in trying to hand them over lost my grip, and the rakes fell every which way. With much fussing and fuming I stooped, gathered the rakes together, and stood and handed them to my father, who was watching me with an even gaze. He took them, paused for a moment without taking his eyes from mine, then deliberately let them go. Watching the rakes scatter on the ground, I burst into laughter. I'd suddenly understood something important—that my striving to gather the rakes (which was, after all, a form of complaint) had served only to make an easy task difficult. They were, after all, only a bunch of rakes, and we were but a man and a boy, working in a garden. So why make a big deal out of it? Why not enjoy ourselves?

Years later I came across the same joke, in an account of the Zen master Ryutan and his student Tokusan:

> Tokusan went one night to Ryutan to ask for his teaching. At last Ryutan said, "It is late; you had better go back." Tokusan made his bows, lifted the blind and went out. Seeing how dark it was outside he came back in, and said, "It's dark out there." Ryutan lit a lantern [a candle with paper round it] and handed it to him. Tokusan was about to take it, when Ryutan blew it out. At this Tokusan was enlightened.

Ryutan's point (in part; in whole it is equal to the universe) was that the student was making too much of the dark. Our fears of the dark and our love of light are ours alone; to God, darkness and light are the same, and if we are to live with natural ease in the universe they must be the same to us, too. If we aspire to make ourselves worthy of dialogue with a "superior" extraterrestrial intelligence, we will need to comprehend that this kind of understanding counts for more than rocket ships, books, or bombs.

So why did my son laugh in his sleep that night? Because he thought of something funny, I suppose. What was it? I don't know, but I'll bet it involved an incongruity. Perhaps he was thinking of one of his many word games, as when he calls a nose a toe, or a man a big lump of oatmeal. Children love word play; it reassures them that words are only words and not things, and rehearses skills taxed by the considerable burden of learning a first language. (The average child memorizes four to eight words a day, accumulating a vocabulary of eight to fourteen thousand words by age six.) Perhaps he dreamed of something physical—a man trying to catch a greased pig, say—and laughed at the disparity between that man's aspirations toward grace and his sadly imperfect actions, and was amused to reflect on his own struggles each day to make his body do what he wanted it to do. (Belly flops can be funny, if the diver leads us to expect something better; a *perfect* dive is funny only if we have been led to expect a belly flop.) Or perhaps he simply dreamed of being tickled. (The gigantic adult menaces the child physically, but the outcome is only a gentle tickle, and so the child laughs.)

Does all this explain humor? Not very adequately, I'm afraid. But it may suggest how humor invokes the darkness of the unknown, while we in our little circle of light whistle and fidget and laugh. Half of that darkness lies outward, in the vast universe; from a cosmic perspective, I suspect, a State of the Union address or an advertising campaign is as funny as an Amos and Andy skit. The other half lies within, where laughter echoes down unexplored corridors of the mind. We laugh when suddenly reminded of how little we are, and how little we know. And that is why we stay young so long as we can laugh, and why every child's laughter is our own.

Death Trip

It is very beautiful over there.

> —Thomas Edison, on his
> deathbed, describing a
> vision of the hereafter

"This is eternal bliss," I thought. "This cannot be described; it is far too wonderful!"

> —Carl Jung, describing a heart
> attack that nearly killed him

Lately we've been hearing that it's good to die. Testimony to this effect comes from the growing numbers of people who have "died" (which is to say that their heartbeat and breathing stopped) and then been revived. Survivors of these "near-death experiences," or NDEs, typically say that they felt themselves rushing through dark space, saw their lives pass before their eyes, and then entered a realm of light where they encountered deceased relatives or friends. The prevailing emotion, they maintain, is ecstasy. A nationwide Gallup Poll conducted in 1982 found that fully a third of the eight million Americans who reported having a near-death experience "recall being in an ecstatic or visionary state." Kenneth Ring, a psychologist at the University of Connecticut who interviewed one hundred two persons who nearly died, says NDEs evoke "a sense of the most profound peace and well-being that is possible to imagine." Some find their flirtation with death so blissful that they get a bit grumpy about returning to life. "Why did you bring me back, Doctor?" one complained. "It was so beautiful!"

What we have, then, is a body of anecdotal evidence indicating that many who come close to death find the experience illuminating and ecstatic. NDE reports are rather consistent in this regard, though they come from individuals of many different ages, nationalities, and religious backgrounds. As one might expect, a few idiosyncrasies emerge: A South Asian Hindu near-death pilgrim ventured to heaven on the back of a "bespangled cow," while an American counterpart hailed a taxicab; and although modern NDE witnesses talk of being bathed in pure white light, a poor Essex farmer named Thurkill, who nearly died in the year 1206, was obliged to make his way through a more traditionally biblical landscape, where he encountered an icy salt lake, a scales where souls were weighed, a nest of piercing stakes and thorns, and a fiery corridor leading to hell. But one is impressed by the overall uniformity of the many NDE reports that describe a rush through darkness, then heavenly light everywhere, a review of one's life, an encounter with the departed, and what Dr. Raymond A. Moody, whose books have drawn widespread public attention to the NDE phenomenon, calls "intense feelings of joy, love, and peace."

What does it all mean? If NDEs provide a glimpse of life beyond death, then they present us with the prospect of a parallel universe, closer at hand than the stars in the sky. And if they tell us nothing about an afterlife, they still may constitute evidence of a harmony between mind and nature extending to the very horizons of mortal existence. In the zone near death falls the shadow of a great mystery. But has this mystery to do mainly with the mind, or with the universe?

The most obvious message of the NDE reports—that death is nontraumatic—is not news. Doctors have been saying as much for years, though few outside the medical community would listen. More than a century has passed since the Canadian physician Sir William Osler, in a study of some five hundred deaths, concluded that only eighteen percent of the dying suffered physical pain and only two percent felt any great anxiety: "We speak of death as the king of terrors and yet how rarely the act of dying appears to be painful," Osler observed. More recently, the American physician Lewis Thomas noted that in all his years of practicing medicine he had witnessed but a single agonizing death, and that from rabies. Certainly a *cause* of death can be disagreeable—it is no fun to have lymphatic cancer, heart disease, or multiple sclerosis—but physicians who regularly tend to the dying agree that death itself is not all that unpleasant.

But what intrigues people about the NDE phenomenon is, of course, not just its emollients against the prospective pain of death, but the tantalizing possibility that near-death experiencers are bringing back glimpses from the great beyond—that, to put it bluntly, they have caught sight of heaven. Those who embrace this view stress that the NDE scenario accords with traditional conceptions of paradise as a luminous domain where we encounter the dearly departed. But however tempting it may be to believe in eternal life, and without pretending to render judgment on the validity of this ancient and widely held belief, it must be admitted that the near-death experience does not by any stretch of the imagination constitute proof that it is true.

The most telling objection to the notion that NDEs represent visions of an afterlife arises from the fact that they closely resemble reports, not of death, but of traumatic experiences that *threaten* death. A cogent study that bears on this point was conducted late in the nineteenth century by Albert Heim, a Zurich geology professor and alpinist who interviewed mountain climbers, masons, and roofers who had survived potentially fatal falls. Heim found that their accounts contained a number of common elements that turn out to be quite similar to modern reports of near-death experiences—a sense of euphoria and calm, a review of one's past life, and a vision of intense light much like a glimpse of paradise. "There was no anxiety, no trace of despair, no pain," Heim noted, "but rather calm seriousness, profound acceptance, and a dominant mental quickness and sense of surety. . . . Reconcilement and redeeming peace were the last feelings with which they had taken leave of the world and they had, so to speak, fallen into Heaven." Heim himself had fallen from an alpine glacier, while climbing at an altitude of 5,900 feet one day in 1871. "I saw my whole past life take place in many images, as though on a stage at some distance from me," he recalled. "I saw myself as the chief character in the performance. Everything was transfigured as though by a heavenly light and everything was beautiful without grief, without anxiety, and without pain."

Now, a climber falling from a cliff is not dead. He is not even ailing. He is fully fit, and is "near" death only in the sense that he has every reason to expect that he is about to die. If, as we have seen, the mental transfigurations he experiences while falling closely resemble modern near-death accounts, then the NDE phenomenon tells us about trauma, not death. And if it doesn't tell us about death, it doesn't tell us about life after death, either.

It appears likely, then, that the physiological basis of near-death experiences is stress. As I mentioned in the previous chapter, the human nervous system responds to threatening situations by releasing a deluge of chemicals into the bloodstream. These chemicals include polypeptides that attach to endorphin receptors in the brain, the same receptors to which morphine and the other opiates bind themselves; when they are activated they result in reduced sensitivity to pain and a sense of euphoria.

Why do NDE accounts so closely resemble the traditional, Bible-tract image of heaven? Precisely *because* these are the visions produced by life-threatening stress. After all, people have been "dying" and coming back to life for thousands of years, albeit in fewer numbers than in today's high-tech operating rooms. And since, as we have seen, their experiences show a remarkable uniformity, it is not surprising that their visions long ago came to be accepted as eyewitness accounts of heaven. If our conception of heaven as a blissful realm of radiant light was itself based on centuries of near-death testimonies, to claim today that heaven is real because our conception of it resembles the NDE reports is to reason in a circle. Therefore I agree with Dr. Moody when he writes that "we are no closer to answering the basic question of the afterlife now than we were thousands of years ago."

But this is not to say that we have drained all mystery from the near-death experience. On the contrary, once we have dispelled the myth that NDEs shed light on the question of whether there is an afterlife, we are left with a greater riddle: Why is it that a human being's encounter with death should most often be attended, not by grief and despair, but by a sense of illumination and ecstasy?

So far as we know, Darwinian evolution is the sole mechanism that determines the genetic endowment of human beings and other living organisms. Random genetic mutations create unique individuals within each species;

natural selection sometimes favors the survival prospects of these atypical individuals; and those who survive long enough to reproduce may contribute their genes to future generations, who inherit the new characteristics that better fit them to their environment.

We can readily understand how Darwinian selection could have worked to produce the stress response: There is survival value in reacting to danger with a blast of adrenalin, which accelerates both mental and physical performance, and with natural painkillers, which by dulling pain enable the threatened individual to ignore his injuries and concentrate instead on taking actions that may save his life.* We are far more likely to be the descendants of young men and women who responded to attack with strength and clear-headed resolve than of those who succumbed to panic and were eaten. Similar benefits of the stress reaction may be identified in other life-threatening situations, from near-drowning to getting lost in the woods.

But what survival value can there be in believing, at a moment of intense stress, that we have entered into an ethereal realm of light, where we encounter the spirits of the dead and watch our lives pass in review before our eyes? These visions would seem, if anything, to distract our attention from the immediate task of surviving a brush with death. And to what extent can Darwinian selection serve to affect our experiences at the very extremity of stress, when

*Many victims of grizzly bear and shark attacks recall that instead of being preoccupied by pain, they experienced a detached state of mind that enabled them to assess their situation with some degree of objectivity. Presumably these changes in their mental state made them better able to deal with the attack and thus enhanced their chances for escape. The way to survive attack by a Great White Shark, for instance, is to relax and not struggle, so that the shark has an opportunity to feel your shape and determine that you are not one of the many fishes it finds tasty. This calls for considerable presence of mind, but divers and surfers who managed to go limp in the shark's jaws have survived to tell the tale.

the heart and lungs have stopped functioning and the odds of survival become vanishing small? If there is any point at which natural selection ought to have *no* further effect, certainly it is at the moment of death. Why, then, is there anything pleasant about dying?

Undeniably, we have a lot to learn about why we die in the first place. We've all heard about people who died once they have lost their reason to live. An old man from Ceylon told me that he used to resent the British civil servants who lived high on the hog in his native land, retiring while still young to sit on the verandas of their grand homes sipping gin-and-tonic, until he observed that most, having realized their fondest ambitions, were dead within a decade. Statistics support the notion that we may be able to exert an influence over the hour of our death: Researchers at the University of California, San Diego, reported in 1990 that elderly Chinese-American women were less likely to die in the week preceding the Harvest Moon Festival than in the week after, when their death rate increased by a third; apparently they were in effect postponing their demise (from stroke, cancer, and heart disease in particular) until after the holidays. "These results are certainly consistent with the idea that there is such a thing as a will to live and that it makes a difference in how long you live," said one of the researchers.

A clue to this mechanism may be found in evidence that near-death experiences tend to be cast in terms of each individual's deepest concerns. Consider, for example, that while most NDErs say they communed with family members (presumably because family is important to most of us) for intellectuals the experience can be much more abstract. The English philosopher A. J. Ayer, who in life wrestled with the concepts of space and time, found himself doing much the same thing when his heart stopped for four long minutes during a bout of pneumonia. Ayer writes that he encountered what he called "the government of the universe."

> Among its ministers were two creatures who had been put in charge of space. These ministers periodically inspected space and had recently carried out such an inspection. They had, however, failed to do their work properly, with the result that space, like a badly fitting jigsaw puzzle, was slightly out of joint. A further consequence was that the laws of nature had ceased to function as they should. I felt that it was up to me to put things right. . . . It then occurred to me that whereas, until the present century, physicists accepted the Newtonian severance of space and time, it had become customary, since the vindication of Einstein's general theory of relativity, to treat space-time as a single whole. Accordingly, I thought that I could cure space by operating upon time.

Hobard Jarrett, a distinguished English professor with whom I used to teach at Brooklyn College, was once aboard an airliner that plunged thirty-four thousand feet before narrowly averting a crash; he tells me that as the plane dived toward the earth his mind was flooded with lines of Shakespeare's poetry. Albert Heim while falling from the glacier worried that he would not be able to deliver a university lecture scheduled five days hence. (Though swathed in bandages, he gave the lecture on schedule.)

Many eerie stories suggest that some have foreseen their deaths. The physicist Heinz Pagels repeatedly dreamed that he would die in a fall. He wrote about this recurrent dream in the concluding paragraph of his book *The Cosmic Code*, published in 1982: "In cold terror I fell into the abyss. Suddenly I realized that my fall was relative; there was no bottom and no end. A feeling of pleasure overcame me."

Six years later, on July 24, 1988, at the age of forty-nine, Heinz stepped on a loose rock and died in a fall, while descending from Pyramid Peak, Colorado.

I am not saying we can see into the future. (There is nothing supernatural, for instance, about a lifetime climber like Pagels anticipating that he might die during a climb.) I *am* suggesting, however, that it is possible to conceive of a suitable death for ourselves, in much the same way that we endeavor to fashion a suitable life. "As I choose the ship in which I will sail, and the house I will inhabit, so I will choose the death by which I leave life," said Seneca the Stoic.

What are we to make of all this—of Heim the geologist believing, in what he thought were the final moments of his life, that he had "fallen into Heaven," or Jarrett the English professor thinking of Shakespeare and John Donne as he plunged earthward in a crippled airliner, or the insouciance of the elderly Chuang Tzu, who when asked by his disciples what sort of arrangements would be appropriate for his funeral, replied, "My coffin will be Heaven and Earth; for the funeral ornaments of jade, there are the Sun and Moon; for my pearls and jewels, I shall have the Stars and Constellations; all things will be my mourners. Is not everything ready for my burial?" Or of Heinz Pagels, writing of his dream of death, "I realized that what I embody, the principle of life, cannot be destroyed. It is written into the cosmic code, the order of the universe. As I continued to fall in the dark void, embraced by the vault of the heavens, I sang to the beauty of the stars and made my peace with the darkness." If there is, as Epicurus believed, "Nothing to fear from God; nothing to feel in death," why not?

I once put this question to Lewis Thomas, who has proposed that the entire terrestrial biosphere resembles a single, unified organism akin to a living cell. "Perhaps the whole system selects for it," he replied.

> I don't know how that would work, but if you were trying to develop a complicated system with a whole lot of different species, as many different kinds of creatures as exist on this planet, and have it work together on this planet as one system in a coherent way where everything depended on everything else, you would need some mechanism that made dying and death acceptable.

In his book *The Medusa and the Snail* Thomas wonders how it came to pass that death is usually painless. "Pain is useful for avoidance, for getting away when there's time to get away, but when it is end game, and no way back, pain is likely to be turned off, and the mechanisms for this are wonderfully precise and quick," he writes. "If I had to design an ecosystem in which creatures had to live off each other and in which dying was an indispensable part of living, I could not think of a better way to manage."

Perhaps we have underestimated the role of harmony in biological evolution. Popular accounts of Darwinism stress fierceness and competition, but for an organism to be "fit" means not so much that it dominates others, but that it is attuned to its environment. Harmony implies communication, and we are beginning to discover that nature is replete with communications channels of great variety and subtlety: Bees communicate by dancing, fire ants by emitting odors; and when a Douglas fir is infected by beetles it emits an allochemical that prompts neighboring firs to produce the insecticide-like substance they will need to ward off the same pests. Considering the enormous number of communications links ingrained in the vast tree of evolution, it may not be unreasonable to suppose that life on Earth resonates with internal and external harmonies as yet unnoticed by science. If so, for human beings to establish interstellar communications links would be less an innovation than a perfectly natural extension of a biological tradition.

It just may be that humans and other organisms are selected in part on what might be called aesthetic grounds, so that our ancestors tended to survive, not solely because they were good at hunting and gathering and agriculture and running away from trouble, but also because they felt that they belonged here—were able to enjoy life, to resonate with the world. Perhaps the bliss we experience when death approaches is a kind of major chord played on the nervous system by the plectrum of stress, a final note that bespeaks our resonance with the wider world, and the message of an easy death is that, in some uncomprehended way, we really do belong in the universe.

If so, death is a cosmological event. Stretching back through time are ties that bind us to all that there is— unbroken threads that tether our lives to all prior earthly life, link its chemistry to the ancient roilings of the molecular interstellar clouds, and implicate their atoms in collaborations of quanta set loose at the birth of the universe. When we inquire into the mysteries of the cosmos—of its birth and death, or our own—we set this old web humming. We have as yet heard but a fraction of its song. We listen for it in the waves on the shore, in the sound of the wind through the branches of the ancient forest, and with radio telescopes trained on the stars.

PART THREE

Things That Go Bump

Name now our names, praise us. We
are your mother, we are your
father. Speak now:
    "Hurricane,
    Newborn Thunderbolt, Raw
        Thunderbolt
    Heart of Sky, Heart of Earth,
    Maker, Modeler,
    Bearer, Begetter . . ."
        —*Popol Vuh*, The Mayan
        book of Creation

Thunderbolt steers all things.
    —Heraclitus

Ever since Darwin—since well *before* Darwin, actually—
biological evolution has been portrayed as a pageant of
steady progress from simpler to more complex life forms,
with human intelligence representing its ultimate attain-
ment. So viewed, the biosphere resembles a marvelously
smooth-running machine, its wheels grinding slowly to spin
blue-green algae into carp, carp into *Therapsid* and so forth,
until an intelligent creature finally rolls off the assembly line.

Understandably, the doctrine that evolution progresses
toward intelligence has long been popular among *Homo
sapiens*, whose chosen species name means "wise" and who

naturally were pleased to imagine that billions of years of evolution, rather than being blindly purposeless, could be vindicated for having finally built something as magnificent as the human brain. As Alexander Pope put it, in the first epistle of his *Essay on Man:*

> *Far as Creation's ample range extends,*
> *The scale of sensual, mental pow'rs ascends;*
> *Mark how it mounts, to Man's imperial race . . .*

The fossil record, however, provides scant support for a gradualist and progressive view of evolution. It presents a picture, not of orderly ascent toward ever higher forms, but of unpredictable tumult and change. Consider the ice ages. Any inquiry into the origins of human intelligence—the only example from which we can as yet extrapolate in theorizing about how extraterrestrial intelligence might have emerged—must take into account that the period during which our ancestors' brains abruptly enlarged, quadrupling in size in less than three million years, coincided with an epoch of remarkable climatic oscillations, when glaciers gripped a quarter of the earth every one hundred thousand years or so. Unless this was a coincidence, it appears that *our* intelligence, at least, emerged not from gradual evolution in a stable environment, but from the impetus of unforeseeable, large-scale changes in the environment.

If we enlarge the time scale and look back over hundreds of millions of years, we find evidence of even more traumatic changes rending great holes in the evolutionary tapestry. Long periods of relative stasis, it appears, were punctuated by spasms of extinction that cleared the way for sudden bloomings of new species. It is becoming clear that repeatedly throughout history something terrible has happened to our planet, something that altered the global environment and thus doomed the majority of the exquisitely well-adapted creatures that had flourished in the old climate. Novelty, it seems, most often arises from the ruins of what had been a virtually perfect world, and we owe our existence not entirely to the excellence of our ancestors, but also to their destruction.

Missing from the progressive paradigm was an appreciation of the significance of catastrophic change. The historical reasons for this oversight are not difficult to identify. The nineteenth-century evolutionists (of whom Darwin was only one; he contributed not the idea of evolution but the mechanism, natural selection, by which it works) were opposed by catastrophists, who maintained that the earth was only a few thousand years old. The catastrophists argued that the earth's brief history was fraught with floods, earthquakes, and volcanic eruptions capable of depositing thousands of layers of geological strata almost overnight. The evolutionists, for their part, rallied around the standard of gradualism, which held that the strata had been laid down evenly over billions of years, by gentle rains, easygoing rises and falls in sea level, and other incremental processes much like those we still see operating today. The victory of Darwinism thereby became a victory, too, of gradualism over catastrophism. As Darwin writes, in the conclusion of his *Origin of Species*, "We may feel certain that the ordinary succession by generation has never once been broken, and that no cataclysm has desolated the whole world. . . . And as natural selection works solely by and for the good of each being, all corporeal and mental environments will tend to progress towards perfection."

Only in recent years have geologists and paleontologists begun to grasp the importance of catastrophe in our planet's history. The theory of "punctuated equilibrium,"

postulated by the paleontologists Niles Eldredge and
Stephen Jay Gould in 1971, asserts that evolution proceeded not gradually, but in fits and starts, with long
periods of stasis interrupted by explosions of new life
forms. The geological record suggests that sudden prolif-
erations of new species were made possible by massive
dieouts, which in turn may have been caused by devastating
impacts of extraterrestrial objects. The result of all this
research has been the rise of a new catastrophism. Its
implications go to the very question of human origins, and
thus bear on considerations of where and how often intelligence may have arisen on other planets.

I discussed this issue over lunch at Berkeley one October
afternoon with the geologist Walter Alvarez. Originally
we'd planned to get together the previous Wednesday, but
on Tuesday a major earthquake had struck the Bay area.
Now, a week later, San Franciscans were still walking
around in a daze, as if seeking their sea legs, while after-
shocks every few hours set the ground to rolling like rangy
swells in a sluggish ocean. Buildings had collapsed during
the quake, as had the upper deck of a freeway, and
sixty-two persons had died. But the effects of the earthquake had not all been bad. People talked of pulling
together, helping their neighbors, and coming to realize
how much they felt a part of the city in which they lived.
"For cultures to be mature there has to be some internalization of a tragic metaphor," Kevin Starr, a historian, told
Robert Reinhold of *The New York Times*. Starr suggested that
the earthquake "gives a certain depth to a culture in San
Francisco that was in terminal pursuit of the trivial."

It was in these circumstances that Walter and I got to
talking about the efficacy of unwelcome change. "When I
was a student I read a lot about the ancient Greeks," Walter
said. "It really surprised me to learn that many of their

great cultural contributions coincided with the collapse of their society during the Peloponnesian War."

"There's a lot to that," I replied. "It reminds me of the monologue Graham Greene wrote for Orson Welles in *The Third Man*. Welles, you'll recall, plays Harry Lime, a racketeer who's selling adulterated penicillin on the black market in Vienna just after the war. It's bad business; children are dying because they've been given this penicillin. Anyway, Harry is confronted by his old friend, played by Joseph Cotten, in the scene on the Ferris wheel, and Harry says something like, 'In Italy for thirty years under the Borgias they had warfare, terror, murder, and bloodshed, but they produced Michelangelo, Leonardo da Vinci, and the Renaissance. In Switzerland they had brotherly love. They had five hundred years of democracy and peace. And what did that produce? The cuckoo clock.'"

Walter had become something of an expert on catastrophes. In the early 1970s his work as a geologist took him to a gorge in Italy, near the city of Gubbio in the Umbrian Apennines. Here strata laid down over the aeons have been reared up above ground and tilted conveniently on their side, so that simply by walking down a path one can examine a geological record spanning tens of millions of years. During the weeks that he worked near Gubbio those summers, Walter became increasingly interested in a particular set of strata that dated from the so-called KT boundary—the break between the Cretaceous period and the Tertiary, 65 million years ago, when the dinosaurs died out. ("KT" stands for *Kreide*, the German word for "Cretaceous.") Not only the dinosaurs but many other species met their fate at that time: The *majority* of species were rendered extinct.

The shadow of death is marked in the Gubbio cliffs by a half-inch-thick layer of red clay. Walter chiseled out a piece of this KT clay, took it back to Berkeley, and showed it to his father, the physicist Luis Alvarez. An inventive man—he held forty patents, on everything from a bifocal spectacles to a stabilizing system for videocameras, and once whiled away a stay in hospital by designing a new piece of medical equipment—Alvarez *père* had been working with his son on developing ways of age-dating rock samples. He suggested they try to determine how long it had taken to deposit the clay by examining its content of the element iridium.

Iridium is classified as a "precious" metal, meaning that it is rare. It is rare because it bonds readily with iron: When the earth was still molten most of its iron sank to the core, carrying the planet's original iridium with it, and consequently little iridium remains in the crust. Such was not the case with comets, asteroids, and meteors. Because these objects are small they lack much of a gravitational field, and consequently their heavy metals, rather than being drawn to the core when they formed, remained homogenized throughout them.

The earth accumulates tons of meteorite debris every day, most of it grains of microscopic size; the earth's surface is constantly being bathed in iridium-bearing cosmic dust. The Alvarezes' idea was to use the iridium as a clock. Assuming that the rain of meteorite dust had fallen more or less steadily over the centuries, a slightly higher concentration of iridium in a given stratum would indicate that it had taken longer to form than had another, similar stratum that was poorer in iridium.

The idea seemed promising, but when Walter Alvarez's sample of the KT layer was painstakingly analyzed by two Berkeley chemists, Frank Asaro and Helen Michel, the results were startlingly different from what anyone had expected. The layer of clay coinciding with the death of the dinosaurs turned out to contain not a little more or less iridium, but *hundreds of times* as much iridium as did the layers above and below it. So high an iridium abundance could not have been created by a constant drizzle of cosmic dust over any plausible amount of time. Instead, there must have been a sudden downpour.

After a year of pondering the matter, the Alvarezes hypothesized that a large extraterrestrial object struck Earth 65 million years ago, triggering the KT dieouts. Either a comet or an asteroid (many Earth-approaching asteroids are the hulks of exhausted comets) would suffice. A comet nucleus six miles in diameter that impacted the earth at a velocity of forty-five thousand miles per hour would unleash far more force than an all-out nuclear war. Authorities in mass destruction, of whom there are many in our troubled times, say that while so formidable an explosion would have killed virtually everything within sight, dispatching three hundred mile-per-hour winds across whole continents and sending tsunamis racing through the oceans of the world, its most dolorous effects would have manifested themselves over the ensuing weeks and months. The fireball, they calculate, lofted tons of debris into orbit, producing millions of ballistic missiles, the heat from which, on reentry, set forests ablaze all over the globe. Dust sucked into the upper atmosphere turned the earth dark and cold, while soot from thousands of fires touched off by the blast compounded the damage; the air became sufficiently opaque to eclipse a brontosaur's view of its own feet. If the comet happened to hit an ocean—as is likely, given that four-fifths of the surface of the earth is covered by water— huge quantities of water vapor were injected into the atmosphere, so that impact winter was followed by green- house summer. Nitrogen and oxygen combined in the heat of the explosion to produce a nitric acid rain fatal to marine invertebrate plants and animals, whose calcium carbonate shells are acid-soluble. These and other drastic changes in the climate presumably would suffice to doom many species of plants, killing off some directly and others through starvation.

After lunch I examined a piece of KT strata under a stereo microscope at Walter's lab. At the bottom of the sample was a thick white limestone layer rich in "forams"— *Foraminifera*, the skeletons of one-celled animals shaped like little spiral galaxies, the same organisms whose shells are found in the White Cliffs of Dover. (Forams proliferated so abundantly in the age of the dinosaurs that an entire geological period is named for them: Cretaceous means "chalky.") Bisecting Walter's sample was the iridium-bearing layer, a turbulent streak of frozen trouble, undulating grays going to brick red. Above that came a bland, salmon-colored red stratum; it was inhabited by only a few forams, all members of a single species. "All existing forams are descendants of just a few guys that made it through," Walter said, looking over my shoulder.

A good scientific theory has at least two things in common with a good work of literature. First, it aspires to be *accurate* (or, more ambitiously, "true," as one might say of a poem or a novel). Second—and this is less widely appreciated outside of science—the theory should be *evocative*. The impact theory may well be accurate—the preponderance of evidence supports it—but it also did a good job of stirring up scientists' emotions. People care about the history of life on our planet, and when you present a new idea of how millions of species met their doom, you get their attention. It was the emotional force of impact theory, as much as its intellectual rigor, that got astronomers, paleontologists, volcanologists, atmospheric scientists, geologists, physicists, and chemists working and thinking about it, producing fresh ideas and evidence pro and con.

Geologists in particular had reason to be grateful for the upheaval. So long as our planet's past had been presumed placid, theirs had been a tedious science, shunned by undergraduates as dull and dirty. "Geology *was* dull in the fifties," Walter Alvarez conceded, as we talked over lunch. "I'm a little bit embarrassed that I started out as a geologist." Then plate tectonics, the once reviled and later resurrected theory that the continents rest on floating plates that move, began to revitalize the field. The relentless grinding of the plate that supports the Pacific Ocean against the one that holds up North America had produced the recent San Francisco earthquake and put geologists on the six o'clock news, their research suddenly perceived as having immediate bearing on questions of life and death. Impact theory brought new excitement to the discipline that had once lulled students to sleep with recitations about dripstone deposits and the chemical formula for hornblende.

The geologists, some of them inspired by impact theory and others scandalized by it, went to work looking for iridium excesses in KT boundary strata at sites elsewhere than Gubbio. (This was an important test: Were the iridium excess limited to a single site, it presumably would have come from too local an event to have caused global extinctions.) They found them—KT strata dug up in Spain, Denmark, New Zealand, on dry land and on the floor of the Pacific north of Hawaii yielded high iridium concentrations—and they found additional evidence of impact as well, in the form of shocked quartz, grains of soot, and tiny spheres of fused silicates like those left behind by nuclear weapons tests.

Meanwhile, others searched for a "smoking gun" crater that would provide direct evidence of the impact itself. So old a crater would long since have been buried in sediment, but could be located by studying deviations in the gravitational and magnetic field—sediments are lighter and less metal-rich than the stone removed by the impact—then dated by taking core samples. In 1990 two geophysicists identified a promising candidate in the Yucatan peninsula, where circular gravitational and magnetic anomalies had long attracted the attention of scientists and mystics alike. Dubbed Chicxulub in honor of the Mayans whose civilization flourished in the Yucatan a millennium ago, this 110-mile diameter crater would be the largest yet found on Earth. Even so, it could account for only half the energy estimated to have been released in the KT catastrophe. Researchers hypothesized that the Chicxulub crater was gouged out by one among two or more objects—a fragmenting comet nucleus, perhaps—that hit the earth simultaneously, and they began looking for other craters. By 1991, signs of candidate craters had been found near Haiti, in Iowa, and in the Soviet Union.

Evidence continued to mount suggesting that impacts may have been responsible, not only for the KT catastrophe, but for scores of the dieouts that dot the earth's long and troubled history. Iridium or other hints of bombardment from space were identified in strata that coincide with the Frasnian catastrophe, 367 million years ago, when giant meteorites punched holes in Sweden and Canada and tsunamis devastated shallow-water ecosystems around the world; at the Permian-Triassic mass extinction, 250 million years ago, when nine tenths of all sea-dwelling species perished; at the Turonian-Coniacian boundary, 90 million years ago, when the oceans all but drowned the continents and the sea urchins were especially hard hit; at the Eocene-Oligocene transition, 35 million years ago, when winter descended and the polar ice caps grew, while the departure of numerous families of tree-dwelling and burrowing mammals cleared the way for the rise of rabbits, dogs, squirrels, gophers, and shrews; and at the mid-Miocene, some 12 million years ago, when the Antarctic ice cap expanded and mammals died out in great numbers.

Critics of the Alvarez impact theory argued that mass extinctions seem to have transpired "stepwise," over the course of millions of years, and they emphasized that a single comet impact cannot produce a gradual dieout. A number of impacts spread over a few million years could have done the job, but no astronomical mechanism was then generally known that could produce such an effect. Certainly one asteroid or comet may hit the earth from time to time, but why might there have been *showers* of such objects?

In search of an answer to this question let us raise our sights from the fossil-bearing strata and eroded craters of Earth, and look out to the limits of the solar system. There, far beyond the orbit of Neptune and Pluto and the hypothetical Planet X, lies the habitat of the comets. Ten trillion billion comets are believed to reside there, in a spherical assemblage called the Oort cloud (after Jan Oort, the Dutch astronomer who postulated its existence). The Oort cloud is big: It begins at about a thousand times the distance of Neptune from the sun, and extends a third of the way to the nearest star. The comets there are not the glowing apparitions we see in astronomical photographs; it takes proximity with the sun to make them sprout tails. Comets in the Oort cloud are naked and unglamorous, each a dirty iceberg a mile or so in diameter, inky as lampblack, a clutch of dirt and snow that has remained frozen since the solar system was born.

Normally the comets of the Oort cloud plod in stable orbits around the distant sun. But once in a while something—the gravitational pull of a passing star, perhaps—tugs at the cloud and perturbs their orbits. Billions of comets, shaken loose by the disturbance, then fall toward the sun. Most of these never make it past Jupiter and Saturn; the gravitational fields of these giant planets either herd them into new orbits in the inner Oort cloud or fling them out of the solar system altogether. But some settle into new, smaller orbits that intersect those of Earth and the other inner planets. Just how many comets are thus escorted into a threatening position is uncertain, owing in part to our ignorance of the true population of the Oort cloud and of all the dynamic variables involved, but as a rough estimate we might expect such a shower to send as many as a billion comets into Earth-crossing orbits, of which anywhere from two to several dozen would hit the earth.

Envision the fatal passacaglia. It takes two or three million years for the perturbed comets to fall into the inner solar system. During this long prelude the night skies of earth very gradually bloom with comets; eventually scores are visible, like some mysteriously multiplying species of celestial paramecia. Nearly all of these comets wander harmlessly past, first growing brighter as they approach the sun and then fading away as they depart a few months later. But then comes one that does not fade, that instead keeps getting larger and brighter, night after night, a dreadful milk-white eye that grows until it embraces the sky, putting the stars to flight and banishing the darkness. *This* comet is coming straight at you, doomed creature.

When it hits, the heavens deliver up hell on earth: Waves shatter undersea coral reefs, dust and soot blanket the sky, water vapor sucked into the air sets off greenhouse heating, acid rain defoliates the forests, and flora and fauna die in wholesale lots, of starvation or poisoning or sheer disaccommodation. Nor is that the end of it. There is likely to be another impact soon, and another, an average of ten or so during the next million years. Creatures that survive one catastrophe expire in the next; by the time the shower abates, the lands of Earth are nearly as sterile as a bacterial colony bathed in penicillin.

This grim scenario fits the fossil record pretty well. Repeated impacts occasioned by a comet shower can produce the "stepwise" patterns that some scientists think they see in the geological record of each extinction event. At the Eocene-Oligocene boundary, for instance, species of plankton appear to have become extinct in four distinct and sudden episodes that took place over some one to three million years. This would be expected, if indeed the extinctions were caused by four or more comet impacts occurring within a comet shower that lasted three to four million years.

Left unexplained at that stage in the development of impact theory was the triggering mechanism that touched off each comet shower in the first place. An obvious candidate was the chance encounter of the sun with another star, but such random celestial flybys occur infrequently. Stars are scarce where we live, out near the edge of the galactic disc—scatter a few grains of sand across all of North America and you have a pretty good representation of the enormous volumes of space surrounding the average star in our precinct of the Milky Way galaxy—and dieouts have occurred more often in the earth's history than chance stellar encounters would permit. Something was missing.

A clue came in 1984, when two University of Chicago geologists, David Raup and John Sepkoski, published a seminal paper suggesting that cosmic bombardments occur *periodically*. Raup and Sepkoski analyzed data on the tenures of some 3,500 families of marine animals. Charted on a graph, the extinction rates of these species showed sharp peaks—dieouts—coming in cycles of every 26 million years or so. "The implications of periodicity for evolutionary biology are profound," the two geologists wrote. "The most obvious is that the evolutionary system is not 'alone' in the sense that it is partially dependent upon external influences more profound than the local and regional environmental changes normally considered."

The suggestion that mass extinctions had been visited upon the earth at regular intervals, as if by the tolling of a cosmic bell, was so outlandish that Luis Alvarez himself did not believe it at first. He stormed into the office of his prize student, the physicist Richard Muller. "Rich," he said, as Muller recalls their conversation, "I just got a crazy paper from Raup and Sepkoski. They say that great catastrophes occur on the earth *every* 26 million years, like clockwork. It's ridiculous. I've written them a letter pointing out their mistakes. Would you look it over before I mail it?" Muller reviewed the evidence, but found it more likely that Raup and Sepkoski were right and Alvarez wrong. When he said so, Alvarez reacted with indignation. The extinctions, Alvarez maintained, were due to asteroid or comet impacts, and astronomers *know* that such impacts occur at random intervals. Muller held his ground. There ensued one of the more interesting combinations of scientific and philosophical discussion in the recent history of science.

"Suppose someday we found a way to make an asteroid hit the earth every 26 million years," Muller suggested to Alvarez. "Then wouldn't you have to admit that you were wrong?"

"What is your model?" Alvarez demanded. He wanted concrete hypotheses, not airy speculations.

"It doesn't matter!" Muller replied. "It's the possibility of such a model that makes your logic wrong, not the existence of any particular model."

"How could asteroids hit the earth periodically?" Alvarez

repeated, his voice quavering with anger. "What is your model?" he repeated.

Muller writes that he thought, "'Damn it!. . . . If I have to, I'll win this argument on *his* terms. I'll invent a model.' Now my adrenaline was flowing. After another moment's thought, I said: 'Suppose that there is a companion star that orbits the sun. Every 26 million years it comes close to the earth and does something, I'm not sure what, but it makes asteroids hit the earth.'

"I was surprised by Alvarez's thoughtful silence," Muller recalled. "He seemed to be taking the idea seriously and mentally checking to see if there was anything wrong with it. His anger had disappeared." Alvarez decided not to send in his letter after all.

Muller's further work on the idea, much of it in collaboration with the astronomers Marc Davis and Piet Hut, evolved into what he dubbed the "Nemesis hypothesis." The idea was that the sun is a double star, its companion—Nemesis—a dwarf in a highly elliptical orbit that brings it close to the sun every 26 million years. When Nemesis swings past the sun its gravitational field perturbs the Oort cloud, touching off a comet shower. The triggering mechanism behind the dieouts had been found—maybe.

To test the hypothesis, Muller and his colleagues set out to find Nemesis. They reckoned that it would have a mass of only about one tenth that of the sun (were it more massive it would be brighter, and astronomers would have discovered it already) and that it must now be near its maximum distance from the sun, inasmuch as the last dieout, that of the mid-Miocene, came some 12 million years ago, roughly half of Nemesis' putative 26-million-year orbital period. They equipped an old thirty-inch telescope in the hills near Berkeley with three computers, consulted a catalog of red dwarf stars, and started taking pictures of their positions with a CCD electronic imaging system. Two images were made of each star, on nights six months apart, when the earth was at opposite sides of its orbit around the sun. If one of the dwarfs were Nemesis, it would lie only 2.4 light years from the sun, much closer than any previously known star, and so would betray itself by a marked shift in its apparent position against the background stars every six months. This displacement, which astronomers call parallax, is caused by the changing position of the earth in its orbit around the sun, and is the basis for measurement of the distances of all stars in our celestial neighborhood.

I talked with Muller one afternoon in 1989 in a redwood grove at the Lawrence Berkeley Lab. He was close to completing his survey of the northern skies; if he found nothing, the next step would be an all-sky survey from the southern hemisphere. "I doubt that the Nemesis hypothesis is taken seriously by most astronomers," he said. "I have mixed feelings about that," he added. On the one hand, Muller said, he would prefer that his theory found adherents among the astronomers, but "on the other hand I'm not really sad that the crowd isn't out there looking for Nemesis, because we'd really like to find it." If an inventory of all the red dwarfs in both hemispheres failed to identify Nemesis, he added, he would abandon the theory and begin thinking anew about what might cause periodic comet showers.

Personally, I was less pessimistic than Muller about the ease with which his hypothesis could be disproved. Our galaxy is known, from dynamical studies, to harbor twice as much mass as the visible stars can account for, and this "dark matter" might take the form of *brown* dwarfs, stars too dim to be seen in visible light at all. If Nemesis is such a star, it would require a special sort of telescope—an infrared telescope in space would do nicely—to detect it. So Nemesis might exist even if Muller's initial search failed to locate it.

After bidding Muller good-bye I strolled in the grove, watching the sun dapple through the redwood branches. If Rich is right, I thought, the sun will never look the same again. No longer will we look at it and say, "There is our sun." Instead we will say, "There is *one* of our suns, the bright one, the giver of life. Out in space lurks another one, a dark star, the star of death."

Impact theory is still the subject of active controversy, and there is no shortage of capable critics who question whether impacts caused any of the great dieouts, whether they have occurred periodically, and whether they could have been caused by a dwarf star orbiting the sun. But whatever may be its fate, the theory has worked to call fresh attention to the old lesson that life owes a debt to death. The prospect of a celestial mechanism behind the dieouts has opened up a radical—and to me, refreshing—new way of thinking about the history of life on Earth.

In Darwin's day, when evolution was thought of as gradual and progressive, the ascent of each new species was viewed as an upwardly mobile process in which ever-better life forms came, however slowly, to take up their rightful place as superior to the less well-adapted forms of life that they displaced. Extinct creatures represented failures, and surviving species—notably ourselves—represented success. To succeed is better than to fail, and so species that survived were thought of as somehow better than those that perished. (Herbert Spencer's term "survival of the fittest" encouraged this assumption; strictly speaking it referred simply to organisms that better "fit" their environment, but to the general public, especially in Victorian England, it connoted physical fitness and superiority.) And so evolution came to be characterized in the schoolbooks as an ascending staircase of ever-better organisms—in other words, as progress. From fish to mammals, from little horses to big horses, and—most satisfyingly of all—from apes to primitive man to *Homo sapiens*, nature was thought to be patiently improving her handiwork.

All this changes utterly once we entertain the notion that evolution dances to a jazzier rhythm than the stately waltz that Darwin and his contemporaries imagined. The key to understanding the new outlook is to appreciate that massive dieouts spell deliverance from the tyranny of the extant. What was catastrophic for the species that expired becomes wonderful for those that survive: They are presented with a Garden of Eden, a clean slate, a frontier of opportunity.

Consider the economics of survival. Our planet offers only so many ways for a creature to make a living. Given a reasonable amount of time in a fairly stable environment, various species will arise and adapt until they have filled every ecological niche. The end result is a steady-state situation in which all the available jobs are held by creatures expert at doing that job. Interlopers need not apply; the chance is small that a new species will appear that can do the job better than the existing species do and thus find an opening in a saturated ecologic market.

Stasis is especially uncomfortable for the freaks—the mutations *within* each species. These are much more common than is generally assumed: On the rare occasion when a species is given an opportunity to flourish without significant competition, mutations are found in surprising numbers. This was the case, to cite one instance, when *Bairdiella,* a small marine fish from the Gulf of California, were introduced to the Salton Sea in 1952. With food abundant and competition nonexistent, *Bairdiella* flourished—the mutations as well as the normal fish. Nearly a quarter of the first spawning of *bairdiella* were visibly deformed. Some were blind, or had no lower jaw, or were hunchbacked, or had two or three spines. As soon as food supplies began to run short, however, the incidence of mutated fish dropped to a few percent; less fit for the environment, the mutants could not compete successfully for food.

But when the environment changes radically, the freaks, some of them, have a chance. If, say, plankton disappear and only fish scales are available for food, a fish that has a deformed jaw may turn out to be better able to feed than are those with normal jaws; the tribe of deformed fish will then multiply, until a freak jaw *becomes* the norm. Now the formerly normal varieties will tend to die out, so that wholesale disappearances of taxa are succeeded by an explosion of strange new forms. Catastrophe sets the stage for the revenge of the nerds.*

All the high-paying, big-animal jobs in the Cretaceous were filled by dinosaurs. They held on to them for 130 million years (which is twice as long as all the time that has expired since their demise) and did them so well as to inspire our enduring respect. The mammals, meanwhile, eked out a living at marginal, furtive, small-animal jobs; in the age of the dinosaurs, no mammal grew larger than a house cat.

Then came catastrophe—a comet intruder, we presume— and the beautifully adapted dinosaurs found that they had no home in a newly altered world. They died out, but the several small mammals that made it through found themselves in vastly improved circumstances. Competition was all but non-

---

*A point that was missed, incidentally, in the film of the same name. When in the movie's climactic scene a "nerd" takes the microphone at a football rally to protest campus persecution of his kind, he tells the "beautiful people," the football players and cheerleaders, "There are more of us than there are of you." The real beauty of nerds, however, is not that they are numerous but that they are different. *Because* they are different they have skills that may prove valuable in a changing world—when, for instance, they leave school and enter the wider world, where the ability to program a computer may ultimately yield more rewards than the ability to throw a football forty yards.

existent; the extinction of most of the earlier species left an enormous variety of positions open, and many a freak mammal found a paradise in the recently ruined Earth. Wild-eyed insectivores took wing as bats, navigating skies abandoned by the extinct pterosaurs; hoofed ruminates grazed on plains newly freed from dinosaur predation; and primates took to the now-safe trees, eventually to be aided in swinging from branch to branch by their opposable thumbs, which were to come in handy in making hand-axes and radio telescopes.

Such was our Eden, and we live in it still—if, as Ben Franklin said of the new republic, on his way out of a meeting of the Continental Congress, we can keep it—but it arose from the violence of a falling star. "Had it not been for the large comet that hit 65 million years ago, mammals might never have wrested the earth from the dinosaurs," Rich Muller writes. And if the mammals had not flourished, who is to say whether intelligence would have appeared? The message of the new catastrophism is that biological inventions like the opposable thumb and burgeoning neocortex arise by celestial accident. If so, we owe our existence—and, therefore, that of intelligent life on Earth—to star-engendered violence.

To search for intelligence elsewhere in the universe is, therefore, to look not for the predictable fulfillment of a progressive plan but for the unpredictable aftermath of a disaster. If impact theory is correct, the most probable abodes for intelligent life are not the placid, untroubled planets, but dangerous worlds fraught with catastrophe. In celestial as in mundane life, the place to seek wisdom is where life is hard.

In a nuclear age, such a fable must bear the cautionary moral that if we press the wrong button we will see what catastrophe looks like from the losers' side. We will not kill off all life on Earth; rhetoric to the contrary notwithstanding, that feat remains beyond our capacity for destruction. We could, however, extinguish many species, especially the land-dwellers highest on the food chain, us in particular. There is a fearful symmetry to the situation, in that the damage we did would harm us more than anyone else. Once the dust had settled, the radiation levels had died down, and the cockroaches had run through their initial rampages, new species would appear. Some of these—the termites, perhaps, gifted with behavioral flexibility and impressive engineering skills—would do quite nicely, their Eden having arisen from the ashes of our demise. *Their* prayers would have been answered. But would intelligence arise among them? And would they be better off if it did?

The Manichean Heresy

Dear Posterity, If you have not become more just, more peaceful, and generally more rational than we are (or were)—why then, the Devil take you.

> —Albert Einstein, message for a
> time capsule

Some races wax and others wane, and in the short space the tribes of living things are changed, and like runners hand on the torch of life.

> —Lucretius

King Belshazzar of Babylon was into some serious partying—he and his several thousand lords, princes, wives, and concubines dancing and carousing and drinking wine from bejeweled goblets and praising false gods of gold and silver and wood and stone—when the moving hand appeared and inscribed the words MENE, MEME, TEKEL, UPHARSIN. Belshazzar's face fell, his knees knocked together—and that was before he knew what the words meant. His countenance darkened further once the translators interpreted the message: "Thou art weighed in the balance, and art found wanting." Needless to say, the moving hand knew what it was writing about: Belshazzar was murdered before sunrise, or so says the Book of Daniel. The year was 539 B.C.

These days (to continue the sermon) we in the technologically developed world have been treating ourselves to
quite a party, and are beginning to sense that the hour is
growing late. We've plundered the resources of our little
planet as if there were no tomorrow, polluted the air and
water, torn holes in the atmosphere, killed off entire species
of living things without even bothering to learn they were
there, and wired up the world with enough lethal weapons
to wreck civilization overnight. It's hardly surprising that we
sometimes wonder whether the human race is being
weighed in the balance, and found wanting.

The fossil record offers little solace. Ninety percent of the
species that ever lived on Earth eventually vanished, many
of them the victims of global catastrophes that in some ways
resemble nuclear war, global warming, ozone depletion,
and the other unpalatable futures we're busily making
possible for ourselves. We are just one more species; what is
to prevent us from joining the silent majority?

As this is a book about science, I will seek to quantify our
quandary in terms of a scientific formula. Called the Drake
equation, after the astronomer Frank Drake, whom we
encountered earlier as the first to run a SETI search, it
represents a thumbnail way of estimating the number of
intelligent civilizations in the galaxy. It looks like this:

$$N = N_* f_p \, n_e \, f_l f_i f_c \, L$$

The Drake equation aims at estimating N, the number of
communicative worlds in the Milky Way galaxy today. It
does this by asking seven questions, represented by the
seven terms on the right side of the equation. They are:

N_*: How many stars are in the Milky Way galaxy? (About
400 billion.)

f_p: How many of these stars have planets? (Perhaps

half, but to be conservative, let's make it ten percent, or 40 billion.)

n_e: How many of these planets are suitable for life? (If the solar system is typical, then each star has about ten planets, one of which, like Earth, orbits in a temperate zone where water is found in all three forms—as liquid, solid, and vapor. There life as we know it might exist. Making the perhaps overgenerous assumption that every such system has one such planet, we estimate n_e at one hundred percent. If so, the galaxy contains roughly 40 billion fertile planets.)

f_l: On how many of the planets where life *can* develop has life actually appeared? (Life began quite early in Earth's history, so this fraction might approach one hundred percent. But even if we estimate it at only one in ten, the yield is still four billion life-bearing planets.)

f_i: On how many planets does *intelligent* life develop? (As discussed earlier, the origin of intelligence is not well understood, and may be due in large measure to chance. If the odds against intelligence are a hundred to one, we still would have 40 million planets with intelligent life in the Milky Way galaxy.)

f_c: How many of these intelligent species acquire interstellar communications technology? (We went from the stone age to radio telescopes in only ten thousand years, so perhaps the leap from intelligence to communications technology typically occurs rapidly. I'll estimate f_c at one in ten, or four million planets.)

L: How long do technologically adept species typically survive?

It is here, at the last term in the Drake equation, that SETI turns most poignant—for two reasons. The first is that since we know of no civilization other than ours, assigning a value to L amounts to guessing at our own prospects for survival. The second is that the solution to the

Drake equation—our best estimate of how many communicative worlds there are in the galaxy today—turns out to be highly sensitive to their average lifetime. If, for instance, technologically advanced societies characteristically endure for ten million years, then our calculations suggest that there are something like four thousand of them in our galaxy right now, and the prospects of finding one via several decades of a SETI effort are not bad. If, on the other hand, technological societies typically last only about ten *thousand* years, then the same equation concludes that there are only *four* in the galaxy today, and SETI becomes a forbidding matter of searching for centuries.

The L clock begins running once a society becomes capable of sending and receiving radio signals across interstellar space; we on Earth achieved this ability a few decades ago, so the local value for L is as yet less than a hundred years. If *that* is typical—if, in other words, we are destined to die out or to collapse into a pre-radiotelescope stage of technology within the next century or so, and if such a fate is typical of communicative worlds—then we are *alone* in the galaxy, and the prospects for SETI are bleak, a situation summed up in a little SETI ditty:

> *Of all the sad tales*
> *That SETI might tell,*
> *The saddest would be*
> *A small value for L.*

We can imagine a number of nonfatal reasons that alien civilizations might go off the air. They might pollute their surroundings with enough radio noise to block interstellar communication (something like that is beginning to threaten human SETI efforts today), or lose interest in

SETI after having listened for a long time and heard nothing, or succumb to a jaded, inward-looking mind-set and turn their backs on the rest of the universe. But what troubles SETI thinkers most deeply is the possibility that advanced civilizations typically fall silent because they self-destruct. If such is the case—if technologically competent species are like cosmic mayflies that live but a day—then SETI is hopeless (and so is just about everything else).

There is something deeply satisfying about delving into doomsday scenarios, and centuries of such scab-picking have produced an abundance of opinions about why there may be no hope for the human race. Four of the more enduringly popular pessimistic scenarios have to do respectively with power, fallibility, aggression, and fate.

The power scenario argues that technology itself promotes self-destruction. To possess high technology is to manipulate power; power can devastate as well as create, and once a species possesses enough power to destroy itself, a single mistake may suffice to doom it to extinction. I call this the *Phaëthon syndrome*. Phaëthon, you may recall, was the mortal youth who tried to steer the chariot of the sun across the sky, a chore normally handled by his father, the god Apollo. The boy lost his grip on the reins and the sun fell from its appointed orbit, killing him and roasting the earth below. (As Ovid tells the story in his *Metamorphoses,* a ruined Mother Earth cried in lamentation, "See my charred hair. Ashes are in my eyes, across my face; have I earned this for my Fertility?")

The more power technology puts in our hands, the greater looms the danger that calamity will result once we lose control of it. Our experience here on Earth to date certainly seems to bear out this point. In less than a century we have increased our energy resources a thousandfold, bringing unprecedented ease to the lives of hundreds of millions of people but so affronting Mother Earth that we have raised the specter of global ecological collapse. During the same period the power of the world's weaponry has increased by more than a million times, owing principally to the proliferation of thermonuclear weapons—which, apropos the Phaëthon myth, work by virtue of nuclear fusion, the same mechanism that powers the sun. In the woeful catalog of lethal technological dangers, from global warming to chemical and biological warfare, nothing yet approaches the threat posed by nuclear weapons. The detonation of even a fraction of them would result in the greatest catastrophe in human history, one that could press *Homo sapiens* and many other species to the brink of extinction and perhaps beyond. As the physicist Kosta Tsipis of MIT observes, "We have the power to inaugurate events totally beyond our control."

At this writing, owing to a welcome thaw in the cold war, the perception is becoming widespread that the threat of nuclear disaster has abated. The correct way to assess a hazard, however, is to multiply the probability of its occurring by the severity of the prospective outcome, and since the severity of nuclear war is for all practical purposes infinite, little comfort is to be taken in marginally reducing the odds that it will happen at a given time and place. For nuclear deterrence to work it must *never* fail, and never is a long time. Imagine that every day of your life you are required to bet on one spin of a roulette wheel. If a certain number comes up, the world will be destroyed; otherwise nothing will happen, and life will go on for another day. Imagine, further, that twenty years ago there were three fatal numbers, and that today there is but one. That means you are statistically safer than you used to be, in that the daily odds of annihilation have dropped from three in thirty-eight (there are thirty-eight numbers on an American roulette wheel) to only one in thirty-eight. Nevertheless, you cannot expect to keep winning forever; sooner or later your number is going to come up, and when it does the penalty will be horrible enough to overshadow whatever satisfaction you may have garnered from living on borrowed time. That is the predicament in which the human species remains, so long as we have anything like our present arsenals of fifty thousand nuclear warheads.

It is too late, however, to hand the reins back to Apollo. Although we can and should reduce the size of our nuclear arsenals, we cannot unlearn the secret of nuclear fusion, or of genetic engineering, or the other varieties of power that threaten our future. We have no choice but to keep driving the chariot; our only hope is to learn to drive it competently. Here the salutary qualities are skill, foresight, and nerve. It may be worth remembering that Phaëthon crashed because he lost not his strength but his composure:

> When the unlucky Phaëthon looked down
> From the top rim of heaven to small and far
> Lands under him, he turned weak, pale, knees shaking,
> And, in the blazing light, dark filled his eyes:
> He wished he had not known his father's horses,
> Nor who his father was, he wished undone
> His prayer. . . .
> Then in quick terror he saw the sky's scattered islands,
> Where monsters rise: Scorpion's arms and tail
> Opening, closing across two regions of
> The Zodiac itself; he saw the creature
> Black, shining with poisoned sweat, about to sting
> With arched and pointed tail. Then Phaëthon,
> Numbed, chilled, and broken, dropped the reins.

That is where we find ourselves today—staring into the frightening blackness of an indifferent universe, face to face with a future in which we must somehow learn how to husband the power of the stars. Do we have what it takes to survive at so dangerous a juncture?

The second pessimistic paradigm, the *fatal flaw*, proposes that we do not. Arthur Koestler made this point in general terms, without worrying too specifically about what our fatal flaw might be: "Evolution has made countless mistakes," he wrote.

> For every existing species hundreds must have perished in the past; the fossil record is a waste-basket of the Chief Designer's discarded hypotheses. It is by no means unlikely that *Homo sapiens*, too, is the victim of some minute error in construction—perhaps in the circuitry of his nervous system—which makes him prone to delusions, and urges him toward self-destruction.

Koestler's formulation may err insofar as other species are concerned: As we have seen, multitudes perished in global catastrophes not because they were imperfect but if anything because they were *too* perfectly adapted, to conditions that abruptly changed. But it makes better sense when applied to human beings, in that we, unlike the other animals, have amassed the power required to make *ourselves* extinct. Maybe we really are too dumb, too shortsighted, too provincial or selfish or loutish or frivolous to manage that power wisely, and are destined to get ourselves into a fix from which not even our vaunted adaptability can deliver us.

If so, I don't see that there is much to be done about our plight. Conceivably we might get in touch with an older and wiser alien civilization that would teach us how to improve our chances of survival, but I doubt that their sagacity would help us out. We already know what we *ought* to be doing—we ought to love one another, treat the earth with reverence, act in ways of which our grandparents and grandchildren would approve—but too often we don't do it. Barring death by cosmic accident, the question of whether we will survive will most likely depend on whether we *deserved* to survive. If we don't, we didn't. In that sense, we are indeed being weighed in the balance.

As the sole species in the universe responsible for the fate of the human species, we should, I think, reject any proffered solution that requires us to surrender our humanity. The application of eugenics—genetically altering humans in order to "improve" their dispositions—is one such alternative. Another is to abdicate our responsibilities to an alien or artificial intelligence, as in the plot of the science fiction film *The Day the Earth Stood Still,* which depicts an intelligent species that has delivered a measure of its destiny into the hands of robots irrevocably programmed to subdue or destroy anyone who commits a violent act. Solutions like these might improve our chances of success, but at a cost of rendering the victory hollow. Were the world's best engineers to craft a "perfect" humanoid, a being free from all human error and frailty, and were this gleaming prototype set free to roam the streets, I suspect that a mob would promptly set upon it and tear it to pieces. We may not be perfect, but we are who we are, and survival is worthless if purchased at the price of our identity as human beings. What shall it profit a species to gain the whole universe, and surrender its soul?

Apocalyptic *fatalism,* the cruelest of all imaginable roads to ruin, postulates that our demise is predetermined and so cannot be forestalled by anything we do or think. Fatalism is popular among religious fundamentalists who assert that we need not worry about the long-term future of our species because there isn't any. Reasonably harmless so long as it is confined to prophets in sandals and sandwich boards, apocalyptic fatalism can be dangerous in the corridors of power. James Watt, President Reagan's Secretary of the Interior, told a Congressional committee that Americans need not concern themselves with the long-term consequences of their environmental policies; "I don't know how many future generations we can count on before the Lord returns," he said. Reagan himself entertained the belief that newspaper headlines fulfilled the prophecies of ancient books predicting the imminent end of the world. Call me a nervous Nellie, but it makes me uneasy when decisions that affect the future of the global environment are being made by people who think the planet won't last much longer anyway.

Apocalyptic fatalism has its roots in the religious opinion that Man is unworthy of God, a view readily corrupted into the heretical conviction that Man is unworthy of existence itself. (I call this heresy because it permits us to abdicate responsibility for the welfare of our fellow creatures and our descendants, and if that's not a sin, I don't know what is.) But fatalistic prognostications have proliferated in secular circles as well. Thirty years ago the English physicist C. P. Snow predicted that nuclear war was imminent, "adding," as Charles Krauthammer recalls, "that his view was not a matter of opinion or speculation, but scientific certainty." In 1968, the biologist Paul Ehrlich predicted that by 1983 the American wheat harvest would have dropped below 25 million metric tons, due to pollution, overpopulation, and pesticides, and that food rationing would have been imposed. (The 1983 U.S. wheat crop surpassed 76 million tons.) The Club of Rome, in a widely quoted study based on sophisticated computer models, predicted in 1972 that the world would run out of gold, silver, mercury, and tin by the year 1990; that hasn't happened, either.

My intention in taking these prognosticators to task is not to belittle their effort, but to point out how hard it is; as the physicist Niels Bohr remarked, "It is very difficult to make an accurate prediction, especially about the future." Human affairs are hard to predict because human beings are adaptable and creative, and these qualities do not lend themselves to computer forecasts. All rising curves that show unwelcome trends in human affairs—whether of population growth, mineral depletion, or CO_2 in the atmosphere—will approach infinity if extended far enough, but it is we who dictate the curves and not vice versa. Intelligence renders the future uncertain for better as well as for worse; it is no more realistic to assert that we are riding hidebound toward inescapable doom than to insist that our species is assured of a bright and cheerful future.

The fourth argument against our long-term success as a species—the most ominous one, in my view—maintains that we are held hostage by our own aggressiveness. It depicts nature as *red in fang and claw,* as the Victorians used to say, and attributes the ascent of Man to Man's ruthlessness. Ruthless we indubitably are; neither cottonmouth moccasin nor great white shark nor typhoid bacillus can hold a candle to our status as the most efficient gang of killers, torturers, and exploiters this world has yet produced. And, dangerous though we are as individuals, more threatening yet are our nation states, which arose from tribes that made their mark by making war on one another. Nations have drawn stoutly defended boundaries all over the geometrically unbounded surface of the planet, and their conduct toward one another is lawless and high-handed to a degree that, were they individuals, would warrant their incarceration. Slight is the hope, we may well fear, that lasting peace can be forged among agencies so arbitrary, barbarous, heartless, and hypocritical as are nation states comprised of human beings.

The view of nature as red in tooth and claw can be generalized to the interstellar scale, with dismaying implications. If *Homo sapiens* owe their domination of Earth to their malevolent genius for violence, then our example suggests that any species that rules its planet is presumptively too vicious to keep the peace. Advanced civilizations therefore may be expected to self-destruct simply because they are in the destruction business; having lived by the sword, they die by the sword. This grim possibility can be elevated (if that is the term) to the level of star wars: One can argue that if there are many civilizations in a galaxy, some hostile and some peace-loving, the hostile ones will have conquered the peaceful ones, so that any society from which we receive a message is by definition suspect of hostile intent. If the Milky Way is ruled by jackboots and war wagons, we'd be lucky to find ourselves alone in the galaxy (though destined to kill ourselves off anyway).

I fear there may be some substance to this argument, but would argue that hope may yet shine through its dark clouds. Here on Earth we find that violent individuals can become more peaceable: When times change the pirate may settle down and buy himself a governorship, the highwayman don a badge, or the drug lord turn his energies to investing in mutual funds and writing checks to pay his daughter's college tuition. Perhaps something similar can happen to nations, once it becomes clear that relentless militarism is no longer a profitable strategy. Arms races and campaigns of conquest ultimately are like any other growth curve: They cannot go on forever without running into compelling forces that mitigate against them. Where there is life there is hope that peace can come, even to the violent.

If, as I have been saying, SETI presents us with a mirror in which to ponder the potentialities of our fate, it may also provide a way of estimating our chances for survival. A prolonged SETI search that heard nothing would hint that technological development is indeed a high-risk endeavor. If, on the other hand, we found even one alien civilization, its very existence would be cause for optimism: Quite apart from the issue of whether its experience had anything to teach us about survival, the fact that it was out there would indicate that technology, though dangerous, is not invariably lethal.

The literary critic Edmund Wilson used to caution his friends against what he called "The Manichean heresy—giving oneself over to the idea that the fate of the world is in doubt and that the forces of evil can triumph." Manicheanism, founded by a third-century Persian called Mani, "The Illuminator," is a dualistic Gnostic religion that divides the moral universe into a kingdom of God, ruled by understanding, reason, music, and peace, and a kingdom of Evil, ruled by disorder, stupidity, noise, and war. The Manichean heresy to which Wilson referred is the belief that the forces of darkness might win—whereas God rules the Christian universe, and Satan survives only by His forbearance (perhaps because we could not otherwise exercise free will, or, less reverently, because a world vouchsafed from evil would be too simperingly boring for God to tolerate).

Theological considerations about the nature of the heretical are given short shrift in SETI circles—understandably so—and the only honest answer to the question of whether the universe of life is Manichean is that we do not know. But when we are ignorant of the answer to an important question, one way to proceed is to ask which path of inquiry promises best to facilitate learning. The British astrophysicist Arthur Stanley Eddington took this position in the 1920s, when confronted with the scientific riddle of the spiral nebulae. Some astronomers believed that each nebula was a galaxy of stars, comparable to our own; others believed that the nebulae were solar system-sized whirlpools of gas, located in our galaxy, which in turn constituted the entirety of the universe. The former hypothesis could be confirmed if the nebulae were resolved into individual stars, but this was beyond the power of the telescopes of the day; the latter would triumph if spectra of the nebulae showed that they were gaseous—but the spectra, confusingly, were stellar. This meant that the nebulae, if gaseous, were made of a substance as yet unknown. Eddington seized on this discrepancy, and argued for the galaxy hypothesis on the grounds that it was the intellectually more fertile of the two: "If the spiral nebulae are within the stellar system, we have no notion of what their nature may be," he wrote.

> That hypothesis leads us to a full stop. . . . If, however, it is assumed that these nebulae are external to [our galaxy], that they are in fact systems coequal with our own, we have at least an hypothesis which can be followed up, and may throw some light on the problems that have been before us.

SETI is somewhat similar. If we assume that technically advanced civilizations are doomed, we are discouraged both from searching for them with our radio telescopes—having concluded, in our wisdom, that they do not survive—and from envisioning a bright future for our own species. Better to hope for the best, to imagine that intelligence and technical facility are rewarded in the universe at large, and, therefore, to keep our eyes and ears open. He is wisest who remembers how little he knows. Einstein wrote, in answer to a child who inquired of him about the end of the world, "I advise: Wait and see!"

The Library of the
Amazon

In the vast Library there are no two identical books.
>—Jorge Luis Borges,
>"The Library of Babel"

Hell is truth seen too late.
>—John Locke

The rain forests are disappearing, as everybody knows. Twenty-seven million acres of Amazon forest, an area equal to that of New York state, went up in smoke in 1988 alone, while another twelve million acres was cut for timber; a tenth of the Amazon canopy is gone already. Elsewhere in the tropics the situation is worse. A century ago, half of India and a third of Ethiopia was covered by forest; today the figures are fourteen percent for India and less than two percent for Ethiopia. Eight out of every ten trees in Ghana have been cut down, as have three quarters of the Ivory Coast's. In all, perhaps a third of the world's tropical forests have fallen victim to fire and the chain saw, and the rate of destruction is accelerating. In the Amazon basin, an ocean of green nearly as large as Australia, we are witnessing the decimation of the last great rain forest in the known universe.

Massive deforestation brings many ugly consequences—air and water pollution, soil erosion, malaria epidemics, the release of carbon dioxide into the atmosphere, and the eviction of indigenous Indian tribes—but most serious, in the long run, is the depletion of the variety of life. If the burning of the Amazon warrants greater concern than did, say, the deforestation of ancient Greek hillsides to build fortresses and triremes, or the conversion of ninety percent of North America's virgin forests into firewood, shingles, and railroad ties, it is because tropical rain forests are so biologically diverse. Although they cover only seven percent of the earth's land surface, rain forests harbor more than half the world's species of plants, insects, and animals. A pond in Brazil can sustain a greater variety of fish than are to be found in all Europe's rivers; a twenty-five acre stand of rain forest in Borneo may contain over seven hundred species of trees, a number equal to the total tree diversity of North America; Manu National Park in Peru is home to more species of birds than is the entire United States; and a single Peruvian tree was found to harbor forty-three species of ants, a total that approximates the entire ant endowment of the British Isles.

Hundreds of thousands of these species are being extinguished as the forests disappear. Most perish before they have even been identified, much less catalogued and studied. The magnitude of the loss is literally incalculable; as the Harvard entomologist Edward O. Wilson writes:

> The worst thing that can happen during the 1980s is not energy depletion, economic collapse, limited nuclear war, or conquest by a totalitarian government. As terrible as these catastrophes would be for us, they can be repaired within a few generations. The one process ongoing in the 1980s that will take millions of years to correct is the loss of genetic and species diversity by the destruction of natural habitats.

This is the folly that our descendants are least likely to forgive us.

Many people are working to curtail the destruction of the rain forests, but so far they have met with little success. The obstacles are mostly economic. Settlers from the slums of Rio de Janeiro who homestead a few acres in Rondonia can nourish the hope of delivering their children from the iron jaws of poverty. A Malaysian logger can turn a substantial profit by clear-cutting a swath of forest and selling the timber to Japan to be milled into plywood crates and concrete molds. A banker in Sao Paulo can burn off a tract of land the size of a Texas ranch, seed the scorched earth with grass, graze cattle on it, and realize millions of dollars' worth of government-subsidized loans, tax credits, and write-offs in return for having "developed" the land.

With the scent of money in the air, few are deeply moved when urged by northern-hemisphere ecologists and academics to forsake their profits and leave the lovely forests alone. If pressed to address the issue, the profiteers note that such protestations smack of hypocrisy. We in the industrial world, they observe, would not be buying rain forest hardwoods had we not cut down our own trees long ago, nor would Indians in the jungle be slaughtering jaguar, ocelot, caiman, and otter if we did not provide lucrative markets for their skins in Berlin, Paris, and Tokyo. They have a point.

Therefore I want to make a case for preserving the tropical forests that is based neither on high-minded expressions of ecological awareness nor sentimental affection for the plants and animals that are being exterminated, but on the hard-headed economic interests of those who live in the nations that have the forests. What these people want, by and large, is more money. They could use it: The annual per capita income in Brazil is under two thousand dollars, and most nations with rain forests are far poorer than that, and I am not going to sit here at the keyboard of a five-thousand-dollar computer and write that they should not try to do better. The question is which course of action—destroying the rain forests, or preserving them—will provide a more prosperous future for themselves and their children. The answer, interestingly enough, opens out onto a new view of the relationship between mind and nature.

The present approach to rain forest management produces wealth for a few, for a short time. Farming burned-off tracts of Amazon rain forest seldom works for long: Less than ten percent of Amazonian soils are suitable for sustained conventional agriculture; most are exhausted by the time they have produced three or four crops; and many of the thousands of homesteaders who migrated from Brazil's cities to the wilds of the west, responding to the government's call of "land without men for men without land," have already had to abandon their depleted farms and move on, leaving behind fields of baked clay dotted with stagnant pools of polluted water. Nor have the ranchers' fortunes been much more sanguine, except when ranching is supported by government giveaways: To graze one steer in Amazonia takes two full acres; most of the ranches operate at a loss, yielding paper profits purely as tax shelters.* As for logging profits, they are real enough, but fleeting—the rain forest, once destroyed, has nothing more to offer—and in any event the real money is made not by the local loggers and their hands-out friends in the

---

*Although Brazil recently repealed some of its development incentives, in 1990 the government was still subsidizing existing Amazon ranches at a cost to its taxpayers of some $2.5 billion a year. Unsurprisingly, ranchers are prominent in Brazilian political circles, as are timber industrialists in Thailand, Sarawak, Sabah, and the Philippines, where hardwood stands are being cut down at a breakneck pace.

government but by the industrialists of the northern hemisphere, who chuckle over cocktails in New York, Tokyo, and Berlin about how they gulled the rubes in the sticks.

The thrust of my argument is that the rubes are being taken—that they're selling their assets too cheaply, hawking for pennies resources that soon will be worth billions of dollars, cutting deals that make the sale of Manhattan for twenty-four dollars worth of trinkets look shrewd. And I'm not talking about intangibles, like the value of walking on a clean forest floor, breathing the cleansing oxygen of the trees, or listening to birdcalls echo across the canopy. Nor am I going to make the case for tourism, though the long-term financial potential of wilderness tourism is not to be sneezed at. No, I'm talking major profits, hovering on the horizon early in the next century, to be made from the rain forest. If it's still there.

To make my case, I must first call attention to a few developments in computer science, information theory, and genetics.

Throughout the history of science, the way in which we think of nature has been influenced by the tools we use to investigate her. The clock, apex of high technology in Isaac Newton's day, encouraged clockwork conceptions of the solar system. From the steam engine, emblem of the industrial revolution, came thermodynamical models that stressed work, efficiency, and the eventual "heat death" of the expanding universe. And so it is with the computer. Computers are data-processing machines; all they do is manipulate bits of information. Since they do this very well—scientists use computers in an enormous range of applications, from modelling thunderstorms and binary stars to replicating epileptic seizures—one wonders whether natural systems themselves are in some sense information-processing systems.

Like its predecessors, this new outlook is not purely philosophical in its implications; it has practical consequences, too. Specifically, you can make money from it. Just as our forebears earned fortunes from the chronometer and the steam engine, tomorrow's fortunes may be made from information. If that sounds like pie in the sky, consider the word-processing program I am using to write this book: It was developed just over a decade ago by two entrepreneurs working out of a garage on borrowed computer time; last year their company had sales of three hundred million dollars, zero debt, and an eighty-million-dollar annual profit. There's nothing intangible about that, even though the program itself amounts to little more than a few hundred lines of code.

Once we start down the road of thinking about nature in terms of data and computation, two characteristics of computers loom large as potential revolutionizers of our conception of nature.

The first is that computers use *algorithms*. An algorithm is a calculational procedure with an indefinite number of steps, in which the direction taken by each step is conditioned by the outcome of the previous step. All computer programs are algorithms; every time a programmer writes a line of code that says, "If X is greater than Y, then do Z," she is using an algorithm. Algorithms differ from the calculus that traditionally has dominated scientific equations, and the differences have interesting implications for the scientific world view.

The distinguishing characteristics of algorithms are well illustrated by the class of computer programs called cellular automata, invented in the early 1950s by the Hungarian mathematician John von Neumann. The "cells" in such a program are computational entities. Each cell is assigned a set of instructions—an algorithm—that tells it how to respond to the behavior of adjacent cells. A programmer can, for instance, treat the dots on a computer screen as cells, and write a program that tells each dot to turn red whenever a majority of neighboring dots is green, and to turn blue whenever the adjoining majority is yellow; the result is a richly and endlessly changing pattern of color on the screen.

The egalitarian behavior of cellular automata, in which patterns emerge not by decree of a central authority but by the constant voting of many equal entities, has obvious parallels with living systems, from ant colonies and flocks of sparrows to cohorts of stock market traders. Researchers in the field of computer science called "artificial life" use such algorithms to program computerized flowers that grow and blossom like real flowers, and computerized flocks of birds that fly like real birds; they hold "artificial 4-H contests" and give prizes for the most lifelike program. The conduct of cellular automata also resembles the way the brain works: Cells in cerebral cortex, where conscious thinking takes place, are not all hooked to some master organ; there is no one part of the brain that controls all the other parts. Instead, they respond to changes of the potential of adjacent cells. Our thoughts and sensations result from the myriad firings of billions of cells, like patterns emerging on the screen of a computer running a von Neumann program.

Small wonder that scientists debate whether the brain is a computer. I am not going to get into that debate; as I was saying earlier, science does a poor job of answering questions about what something "is." My point is simply that computers offer us an enriching way of understanding life and thought and other natural processes as well. And the history of science and technology demonstrates that fresh understanding can lead to fresh profits; that's why corporations invest in research and development.

The other influential characteristic of digital computers has to do with the fact that they divide the perceived continuum of nature into discrete bits of *information*. Inasmuch as this process works—you can model the explosion of a star or the growth of bean roots on a computer, and if you do the job properly the model will predict how a real star explodes and real roots grow—one is impelled to wonder whether nature might be regarded as made, not so much of atoms and molecules, but of information. This is the great contribution of the computer to contemporary scientific thought, and I will have more to say about it in the next chapter. Here, though, I want to concentrate on the value (financial as well as intellectual) of conceptualizing biological systems in terms of their information content.

Every living thing harbors a wealth of information. The DNA molecule, the basis of all life on Earth, is above all else a mechanism for storing information. DNA data tell embryonic humans how to grow eyes and hands, embryonic sharks how to make sharkskin, chicks in their shells how to form feathers and beaks. By analyzing the structure of the DNA molecule, we can estimate how much information each plant or animal contains. These numbers turn out to be quite large. A humble single-celled microorganism contains about a megabyte of data, an amount that exceeds the content of all the words in this book. The DNA of a more complex organism contains as much information as thousands of books. That's so much data that just to index it, much less understand it, takes an enormous amount of work: To map every gene in the human DNA molecule, the goal of a federal project called the Human Genome Initiative, is expected to consume the efforts of thousands of scientists for some twelve to fifteen years. As Professor Wilson writes, "The power of evolution by natural selection may be too great even to conceive, let alone duplicate."

Some of the data encoded in a creature's DNA have to do with how it gets along in the world: The genes of the spider monkey constitute a textbook in how to swing gracefully through the forest canopy, as our distant ancestors did, while those of the albatross detail how a giant bird can stay aloft on marine air currents for days without flapping a wing. Other DNA data comprise a historical record of how the organism got to be the way it is—how it survived the many challenges it faced in a changing world over millions of years of evolution.

To date we've browsed in only a few pages of the vast genetic library, but even this brief perusal has yielded a lot of useful information. Engineers have drawn inspiration from the infrared receptors on a rattlesnake's nose, from which the heat-seeking guidance system of the Sidewinder air-to-air missile was derived; from the long-range echo sounding equipment of the great whales, which can outperform the sonar sets on nuclear submarines; and from the intricate construction of beaver dams, which outlast human dams. Toxicologists express admiration for the properties of cobra venom, and jetliner navigators say they envy the direction-finding abilities of migratory birds and sea turtles.

The most conspicuous of nature's genetic cornucopias are the tropical plants, each a chemistry set of biodynamic compounds with significant potential benefits for agriculture, energy, and medicine. From the Amazon already has come rubber, indigo, cacao, vanilla, sarsaparilla, chicle, manioc, cashew, and a host of valuable medicines including ipecac, used to treat dysentery, and quinine, the malaria

remedy that has cured more people than any other agent
yet employed against infectious disease. *Curare,* an Indian
arrow poison made from a plant that grows only in the
Amazon, is valued by heart surgeons as a muscle relaxant.
The *mekraketdja* plant is said by the Kayapo Indians of
eastern Amazonia to yield a powerful contraceptive. Co-
caine remains the local anesthetic of choice for many sorts
of eye operations, and has contributed the blueprint for the
manufacture of other local anesthetics, among them pro-
caine, the handmaiden of painless dentistry.

In all, fully a quarter of the prescription drugs sold in the
United States over the past twenty-five years were extracted
from tropical plants. In 1984, American consumers spent
twelve billion dollars on these pharmaceuticals. Yet all these
profits were derived from fewer than fifty among the
millions of plants to be found in the world's jungles and
forests. Of an estimated two hundred fifty thousand species
of higher plants on Earth, only about five thousand—two
percent—have yet been screened for medicinal properties.
A five-year study by the National Cancer Institute, which
will collect and test twenty thousand samples of bark,
roots, leaves, and wood from the trees in Africa and
Latin America to identify drugs useful in treating AIDS
and cancer, will scarcely scratch the surface. There are
perhaps eighty thousand species of higher plants and thirty
million animal species in Amazonia alone. Confronting a
rain forest, the modern botanist stands as humbled by his
ignorance as an astronomer pondering life among the
galaxies.

Largely lost already is the fund of botanical knowledge
commanded by Indian shamans—the "medicine men" so
often patronized in first-world novels and movies. "The
Barasana Indians of Amazonian Colombia can identify all
of the tree species in their territory without having to refer

to the fruit or flowers—a feat that no university-trained botanist is able to accomplish," writes conservationist Mark Plotkin, who notes that "a single shaman of the Wayana tribe in the northeast Amazon, for example, may use more than a hundred different species for medicinal purposes alone." But the Indians are disappearing. Disease, development, and ecological disruption has wiped out an average of one tribe per year since the turn of the century in Brazil alone; many perished before any outsider had even learned their language. And the heritage of the medicine men is dying out among the surviving tribes as well. "Of all the shamans with whom I have lived and worked in the northeast Amazon," Plotkin reports, "not a single one had an apprentice."

So the fires of the Amazon are consuming what amounts to the world's richest natural library. Efforts are under way to preserve some species by removing plants and animals from the forest before they can be destroyed, but these exertions, though salutary, are ultimately as pathetic as those of the bibliophiles who fled the San Francisco fire carrying armloads of books. Few rain forest plants and insects can long survive outside their natural habitat, and as for the larger animals, all the zoos in the world support only about four thousand species, of which fewer than a thousand can be expected to breed in captivity. It might be possible, using some future technology, to extract the DNA of lost organisms from the baked and hardened clay of what was once a forest floor, but this would be like sifting through the ashes of the Library of Alexandria for traces of the lost works of Aristotle, Berosus, or Menander of Tyre. The only way to preserve the treasurehouse of information stored in Amazonia is to let the rain forest live.

If permitted to survive, the forests could deliver up riches far beyond the current calculus of short-term profit and loss. Some of these profits can come from conventional sources, such as the cultivation of herbs. World trade in medicinal plants, for instance, is substantial and growing: The United States alone imports tens of millions of dollars worth of tropical plants annually; just one plant, the rosy periwinkle of southeastern Madagascar, a source of alkaloids used to treat leukemia and Hodgkin's disease, brings in fifty million dollars a year worldwide. Sustained-yield forestry promises profits that dwarf those realized by clear-cutting; if Amazon forest areas designated for clearing were logged rather than being burned—if seedlings were planted to replenish the forests, and logging were conducted in buffer zones around undisturbed tracts of perpetual wilderness—Brazil could earn an additional $2.5 billion annually from the sale of construction timber, fruits, oils, nuts, sweeteners, resins, tannins, and fibers, and its timber profits could stretch on into the future. If instead it continues its present policies, Brazil will repeat the mistakes of Ghana, the Ivory Coast, Haiti, Nigeria, Gambia, Senegal, and Togo—nations that clear-cut virtually all their forests, and today, as a result, confront widespread soil erosion, disease, homelessness, unemployment, and a collapsed timber market. Profits loom large in many other rain forest commodities as well, in enterprises ranging from biofuels and bioplastics (automotive engineers talk of twenty-first-century cars running on plant-grown fuels and made of plant-grown plastics) to butterfly ranching.

Dwarfing all these potential sources of revenue, however, are the profits to be garnered from analyzing genetic data in an information age. The world is rapidly wiring itself into one huge computer complex, and in this environment the most valuable future commodity promises to be hard, fresh data. As Heinz Pagels wrote in 1988:

> A new salient of knowledge is being created. . . . Information, be it embodied in organisms, the mind, or the culture, is part of a larger selective system that determines through successful competition or cooperation what information survives. Information can be encoded in genes, nerve nets, or institutions, but the selective system that promotes survival remains similar.

Information can be transmitted at the speed of light, from computer terminals through fiber optics lines and across satellite networks, to become the common property of scientists, physicians, industrialists, and government leaders around the world. In a great many fields of endeavor, from nanotechnology (the building of molecule-sized machines) to pharmaceuticals, the message is the same—that the wealth of the twenty-first century will be made not in gold, as was the case in the nineteenth century, or machines, as in the twentieth century, but in information.

Early in the industrial age, nations made money from *material* resources; South Africa, for instance, became rich by trading on its assets of diamonds, chromium, and gold. More recently, fortunes have been made from what might be called nations' *cultural* resources; Italy turned itself from the poorest to the third-wealthiest European nation largely by exporting such cultural capital as sports cars, cuisine, and couture. To these assets now must be added the even greater potential riches to be gained from *biological* capital. The wealth of the future, I'm suggesting, lies in the data banks of the natural world.

The Amazonians are sitting on a mother lode of information, and there's no reason why they can't sell it. A royalty on genetic information—like the royalty the American horticulturist Luther Burbank collected on the apples he cultivated—could make the proprietors of the Amazon rich; the key to a cancer cure is worth far more to the world than a million board-feet of timber. If, instead, they destroy the rain forests, throwing away terabytes of genetic data, they will go down in history as wastrels and fools. The choice is theirs.

Or, more properly, ours, for the more the world shrinks, the more it becomes a commonweal. We would all do well to ask ourselves how we are likely to be judged by our grandchildren. It is one thing to use up oil and precious metals to fly aircraft and drive cars and trucks, to build an industrialized world. It is quite another to squander four billion years' worth of the planet's genetic endowment, to tear great rents of ignorance in the potential learning of our descendants, all for the sake of a fleeting profit in rosewood and ply.

The "developed" world was developed by men and women who shared a vision of the future and the courage and determination to make it come true; we live amid their realized dreams, and enjoy the command over nature that ranked high among their aspirations. Now we need new dreams; more of the same won't do. Some can glimpse a future in which the human mind finds fresh resonances in the unspoiled wilderness, where everything alive is held sacred because it all has something to teach us. The Brazil of that future could be a capital of wealth and learning, home of the library of the Amazon, a global nerve center generating new ideas for use in engineering, medicine, and basic research. If we can dream that dream, we can make it happen, and we will earn our descendants' esteem. If we run it into the ground, they will regard us as simpletons, hayseeds, yokels, bumpkins, and clowns. Either way, we're going to get what we deserve.

IT

The world is the totality of facts, not of things.
—Ludwig Wittgenstein

The subject matter of research is no longer nature in itself, but nature subjected to human questioning . . .
—Werner Heisenberg

I'd like to end this book as I began it, by invoking the image of an hourglass or a tree to denote the relationship between the mind and the universe. The nexus of these two domains—the throat of the hourglass, the trunk of the tree—is an active, dynamic region where energy flows in both directions. Sense data are conveyed to the brain from the wider world, but the eye and the rest of the brain, rather than passively recording images, actively select and manipulate them. Perception is an *act;* as the English neuroanatomist J. Z. Young notes, we "go around actively searching for things to see and . . . 'see' mainly those things that were expected." We act, in turn, *on* the outer world, projecting our concepts and theories and manipulating nature in accordance with our models of her. It seems to me that many philosophers have gone astray by assuming that the traffic at the neck of the hourglass goes in one direction only. Thus realists assert that the universe is just as we perceive it (yet the book you are holding in your hands is a black vacuum, with storms of neutrinos howling through it) while idealists say that it's all just thought (yet a falling rock you never saw coming can strike you dead). I'd prefer to set such dogmatic assertions aside, and concentrate instead on the act of observation itself. Specifically, I'm going to outline how a philosophy of science may be constructed from observational data, rather than on more derivative concepts such as space, time, matter, and energy. Such a philosophy would portray the *observed* universe as made not of atoms or molecules, quarks or leptons, but of discrete units ("bits") of *information.*

I will describe this approach as "information theory." The term is usually employed more narrowly, to describe a theory concerned with communications and data processing, but I'm anticipating its expansion into a wider account of nature as we behold her.

Given that our observations represent, at best, only a small and distorted part of the whole, we naturally wonder to what extent we can ascertain what "really" is out there. To this vital question physics has proffered two visions of how mind and nature interact—the *classical* view, ascendant in the nineteenth century, and the more recent *quantum* view. In practice physics employs both: Classical concepts are applied to large-scale phenomena (roughly from the level of molecules on up), while quantum mechanics rules the small-scale realm of atoms and subatomic particles.

The classical outlook rests upon three commonsensical assumptions that like many another decree of common sense are not altogether true. The first is that there is but a single, objective reality to each event: Some one thing happens—electrical current flows through a wire, say, deflecting a compass needle—and while each observer may witness only part of the entire phenomenon, all can agree on exactly what happened. The second classical assumption is that the act of observation does not in itself influence what is observed; the classical scientist observes nature as if from behind a sheet of plate glass, recording phenomena without necessarily interfering with them. The third assumption is that nature is a continuum, which means that objects can in principle be scrutinized to any desired degree of accuracy; observational errors and uncertainties are ascribed to the limitations of the experimental apparatus.

The classical approach fared well so long as physicists concerned themselves with big, hefty things like stones, steam engines, planets, and stars. Such objects can be observed without obviously being perturbed by the act of observation. We know today that the influences are there—when a nature photographer takes a flash photo of a wasp, for instance, the light from the flashgun buffets the wasp a bit, and adds fractionally to its mass—but as these intrusions have no discernible effect on the macroscopic scale, they usually can be ignored. And ignored they long were; classical physics can be *defined* as the physics of objects that are not noticeably altered by observation.

The classical view started to break down, however, once physicists began investigating subatomic phenomena like the behavior of electrons in atoms or the collisions of protons in particle accelerators. Subatomic systems are perturbed by *every* act of observation; to try to count the number of electrons in a cloud of gas by taking a flash photograph of them is rather like counting the number of pupils attending a lecture by blasting them out of the classroom with a fire hose. We can no more comprehend the world of the very small without taking the act of observation into account than we can investigate the destruction of a china shop without paying attention to the bull that did the damage.

Thus arose quantum mechanics, in which the information obtained from observations is seen to vary according to the way the observations are conducted, so that the answers we derive from an experiment depend on the questions we choose to ask. In the quantum world, the classical pane of glass is replaced by an elastic membrane that shudders and flexes at the touch of each observation; peering at the dancing lights and shadows of this soap-bubble interface, we cannot always be certain which phenomena are properly to be ascribed to the outer world and which were stirred up by the act of interrogation.

The erosion of the classical outlook dates from the German physicist Werner Heisenberg's enunciation, in 1927, of the "uncertainty" principle. Heisenberg found that there is an intrinsic limitation to the amount of accurate information one can obtain about any subatomic phenomenon. This limitation arises from the fact that neither we nor anyone else in the universe can observe subatomic particles without interfering with them in one way or another. If we want to determine exactly where a neutron is, we might let it slam into a target (which will stop it in its tracks) or take a photograph of it (which means clobbering it with photons that will send it flying away on a new trajectory), or elect to use some other procedure, but in every case we will have destroyed information about what the neutron might have done had we let it alone. And this situation pertains universally in the quantum realm: To learn one thing about a subatomic phenomenon means to be ignorant of something else. The Heisenberg limitation does not depend on conventional experimental error, or the inadequacies of any particular technology; it is fundamental to every act of observation, whether conducted with sealing wax and bailing wire on Earth or by gleaming machines on the most technically advanced planet in the Virgo Supercluster.

The uncertainty principle makes it clear that on the small scale, at least, the only *un*perturbed phenomena are the ones that go unobserved! The *observed* universe therefore cannot rightly be regarded as having a wholly independent, verifiable existence, since its apprehension requires the intrusion of an observer, whose actions inevitably influence the data that the observation yields. (As to the *un*observed universe we are well advised to heed the counsel of the philosopher Ludwig Wittgenstein, that "whereof one cannot speak, thereof one must be silent.")

At first blush, the realization that we cannot observe the outer world without influencing it might not seem to threaten the classical assumption that there is an objectively knowable universe out there all the same. Classical physicists could (and did) take refuge in the argument that there can still be but one true reality, even if the observer cannot directly access it, just as there must be but one correct verdict in a murder trial even though the jurors can never know all the facts about the case being tried. But the better one becomes acquainted with quantum physics, the more even the simplest physical events begin to look like *Rashomon*, the Ryunosuke Akutagawa story about a rape trial in which each witness presents a plausible but incompatible version of the crime. In the quantum domain, every answer is tinted the color of the question that elicited it.

The famous "dual slit" experiment illustrates how quantum physics upsets the classical assumption of objective reality. The question posed by the dual slit experiment is whether subatomic particles like protons, electrons, and photons are particles or waves. All subatomic particles behave like particles under some circumstances and like

waves under others; physicists use mathematically equivalent particle and wave equations in dealing with them,
depending on which is more convenient in solving a specific
problem. But particles and waves have mutually exclusive
properties. Waves spread out as they travel across space,
and interfere with one another when they intersect.
Particles, in contrast, maintain their discrete, individual
identities—individual particles do not spread out—and
when clouds of particles intersect they mostly fly right past
one another, with a few odd collisions. The dual slit
experiment forces the question: If classical physics is right
there can be but one verdict, either particle or wave.

To familiarize ourselves with the issues involved, let's first
set up the experiment using macroscopic (i.e., classical)
objects. We erect a wall containing two parallel, vertical slits,
place a target behind it, and fire a machine gun at the wall.
After a while, the bullets that pass through the slits will have
inscribed two vertical stripes on the target. If we close off
one slit, we will get one vertical stripe on the target. A
physicist, shown only the targets and a diagram of the
experimental apparatus, will conclude that what we fired
at the target were particles. Now we submerge the wall so
that the slits are half under water, send a succession of
waves toward the intervening wall, and make a target out of
some material that can record wave impacts (beach sand will
do). When each wave passes through the slits it generates
two new sets of waves on the other side of the wall, one
radiating from each slit. Where these new waves strike one
another they create an *interference* pattern—the wave pattern is reinforced wherever wave peaks overlap other wave
peaks and troughs overlap troughs, and is canceled out
where waves meet troughs. As a result our sandy target will
be inscribed with a series of bands. Our referee, shown this

interference pattern on the target, will correctly conclude that it was made by waves.

So far so good. But watch what happens when we venture into the quantum realm. We replace the machine gun with a device that emits subatomic particles—electrons, say—and use as our target a phosphorescent screen that glows when struck by electrons. (That's how a TV tube works.) If we leave both slits open and fire a lot of electrons at the obscuring screen, we find that the target displays an interference pattern. Electrons therefore look like waves—so long as we leave both slits open. But if we close one slit, suddenly we get a *line* on the target; now the electrons are impersonating particles.

This seems strange, but stranger still is what happens if we turn down the emitter power until it fires only a single electron at a time. Now we close one slit, and record but a single impact on the target: Fair enough, the electron is a particle. But if we leave *both* slits open, and fire but a single electron, we get—an interference pattern!

This is exceedingly weird. If we regard the electron as a particle we must conclude, absurdly, that it somehow manages to split in two and pass through both slits, *when and only when both slits are open.* If we regard the electron as a wave, then we must imagine that it somehow folds up and imitates a particle, *when and only when one of the slits is closed.* And the experiment can be made even more mind-boggling: Let's wait until *after* the electron has been fired, then quickly open or close one of the slits *while the electron is on its way.* Here we enter the domain of the so-called "delayed choice" experiments, and again the results are the same: The electron behaves like a particle whenever one slit is open, and like a wave whenever both slits are open.

So long as we cling to the classical assumption that

electrons are "really" either particles or waves, the dual slit experiment results in paradox. This is what makes the experiment so difficult to grasp; as the Danish physicist and philosopher of science Niels Bohr remarked, when a student complained that quantum mechanics made him feel giddy, "If anybody says he can think about quantum problems *without* getting giddy, that only shows he has not understood the first thing about them."

Bohr offered a way to escape the paradox, via what today is called the "Copenhagen interpretation" of quantum physics. We concede that the electron is not "really" either a particle or a wave, but assert that it assumes one or the other costume depending upon how it has been interrogated. Quantum physics thus teaches that the identity of (small) objects depends on the act of observation—that our conceptions of the foundations of physical reality result from a dialogue between the observer and the observed, between mind and nature.

True, quantum physics is confined to the realm of the very small; only recently have physicists managed to write a quantum mechanical description of something as large as a single molecule, and molecules are a billion times smaller than human beings. But this does not mean we can ignore the implications of quantum observer-dependency for the macroscopic world. For one thing, the physics of the minuscule has always commanded particular respect in the philosophy of science, inasmuch as big things are made of small things; surely we have learned something important when we discover that apples are made of atoms. For another, quantum effects do influence the macroscopic world; the sun, for instance, wouldn't shine were it not for quantum tunneling and quantum leaps and various other manifestations of quantum uncertainty. Everything is observer-dependent to some degree.

If, then, we accept that the questions the observer asks influence what he has the right to say about what he observes, we are led to consider that we live in a *participatory* universe, one where the knowable behavior of subatomic systems depends on the methods we employ to study them. Might it be possible to construct our scientific conceptions of the world on the basis of this realization?

I think so. I think, specifically, that both the quantum and the classical approach can be subsumed into the broader paradigm that I am calling information theory— or *IT* for short. *IT* accepts that our knowledge of nature always devolves from a partnership between the observer and the observed; it therefore banishes from science all questions about what things "really" are, and focuses instead on the observational data themselves, restricting models of the universe to what is in fact knowable. All else is regarded as beyond the province of science: If I thump my fist on the table and declare that electrons are particles and not waves, I'm talking philosophy, not science.

At this point the philosophically astute reader, suspecting that I am dressing old philosophies in new clothes, may object along something like these lines: "Is not the position you are staking out here simply the *logical positivism* of the Vienna Circle, those philosophers who dismissed as meaningless all statements that cannot be empirically verified? And are you not perhaps flirting with *solipsism,* denying the independent existence of the universe and making it all depend on your puny observations?"

Well, maybe so, but for the purposes of this discussion I want to set aside all the "isms," and with them the supposition that we human beings sit on some cosmic court of appeals empowered to decide what does and does not exist. My point is simply that scientific statements about the universe, to the extent that they depend on observation, cannot be employed to make statements about what nature is like *independent* of the act of observation. I am *not* arguing for what has been called "quantum solipsism," the assertion that nothing exists except when it is observed: I assume that there are things out there, but I reject as presumptuous any scientific attempt to declare once and for all what they are. The concept of "things" is itself derived from observational data; therefore data are more fundamental than things. What we call facts about nature are inductions from the data, and it is in this spirit that I invoke Wittgenstein's aphorism that the observable universe is made of facts, not things.

Let me first sketch the background of *IT*, then describe how it might be expanded into a philosophy of science.

Information theory may be said to date from the year 1929, when the Hungarian-born physicist Leo Szilard wrote a paper identifying *entropy* as the absence of information. Entropy is a measure of the amount of disorder in a given system. The second law of thermodynamics declares that in any "closed" system—i.e., one to which no energy is being added—entropy will tend to increase with the passage of time. A drink with an ice cube in it is in a low-entropy state. Leave the drink alone, and the entropy increases: The ice cube melts, its water dissipates through the drink, and soon the whole system consists of but one substance, a (watery) drink.

To the thermodynamicists of the nineteenth century, the important thing about low entropy was that it meant you could get *work* out of a system. An ice cube can do some work. It can cool a drink, for one thing, and it can do other sorts of work as well: If Martians were to dispatch a tiny probe to Earth and land it in the drink, they could, if they were clever about it, use the thermal gradient in the drink to recharge the batteries on their space probe. A drink at room temperature in which the ice has melted, however, can do no such work. We can extract some of it, freeze it, and regain the capacity to do work, but this requires that we put some energy into the system. One always must pay to decrease entropy; that's the second law of thermodynamics.

But to Szilard, the interesting thing was that the drink starts out with more *information*. It contains, for instance, several distinct realms—one cold (inside the ice cube), another relatively warm (far from the cube), and other, intermediate thermal domains. As the ice cube melts, the amount of information declines, until at maximum entropy the drink has but a single story to tell: "I'm at room temperature." More entropy, Szilard saw, means less information.

Information has a price; there's no such thing as a free lunch, and every time we learn something about a given system we increase its entropy. The price of information, however, is wonderfully small: To extract one bit of data costs only 10^{-16} of a degree of temperature of heat on the Kelvin scale.* That's a minuscule number—a penny is more than 10^{-16} of the U.S. national debt—and the fact that it *is* minuscule is the reason we can live in an information society today. Low entropy cost means that phone lines don't need to carry high voltages and that communications satellites can run on modest amounts of solar power. It is because information adds so little entropy to the systems we use to transmit it that we can afford to telecast soccer matches

*The relevant equation is
$$S = k \log W$$
in which S denotes the entropy of a given system, W the number of accessible microstates, and k Boltzmann's constant, equal to 1.381×10^{-16} erg/Kelvin. This formula, one of the most wide-reaching in all science, was the work of Ludwig Boltzmann, who decreed that it be inscribed on his tombstone.

around the world, buy books, send electronic mail by computer, and make long-distance phone calls; in each case the cost in entropy per bit of data communicated is low enough to keep the bills manageable.

That is also why we can afford *interstellar* communication. But before getting into all that, let me outline how information theory works, and offer a few examples of how it can bring fresh perspectives to scientific research.

Information theory originally was applied to practical technological problems, such as designing computers and predicting the signal-to-noise ratio of telephone lines. In a typical *IT* equation one begins with a data input *A,* traces what happens to the data when they are manipulated or communicated in a given system *B* (e.g., to what extent data are lost due to noise in a communications channel), and predicts the form in which they will arrive at an output stage *C.* This process has properties that can be quantified mathematically. Claude Shannon of Bell Labs found in the 1940s that the accuracy of any information channel can be improved, without decreasing the data rate, by properly encoding the signal. This discovery, known as Shannon's second theorem, is today employed in many sorts of communications; the clarity of the photographs that the Voyager spacecraft transmitted back to Earth from the remote planet Neptune owed a lot to Shannon. But the ultimate significance of Shannon's second theorem resides in its universality: The theorem pertains to every kind of communications channel, embracing not only telephones and computers but brain circuits and perhaps even the mechanism of biological reproduction. Information theory proffers a common ground for understanding every branch of science, insofar as each involves an input stage (data from the outer universe), a communications or data-processing system (the brain), and an output stage (a scientific theory or hypothesis, which then forms a kind of communications loop when projected back onto nature).

If information theory is to unify science, however, there must be a common language, shared by all the various sciences and applicable to every field of scientific investigation. The key to this language, I submit, is *digitization*, the breaking down of data into *bits*.

The term *bit* is short for "binary digit," the kind of numbers employed by modern digital computers. The binary system expresses all numbers in terms of only two digits, 0 and 1. That makes it much simpler than the base-ten numbering system we learn in school, which requires ten symbols (0, 1, 2, 3, 4, 5, 6, 7, 8, and 9). Here is how the first five digits of the familiar ten-based system translate into binary numbers:

Decimal number	Translation	Binary equivalent
0	0×2^0	0
1	1×2^0	1
2	$(1 \times 2^1) + (0 \times 2^0)$	10
3	$(1 \times 2^1) + (1 \times 2^0)$	11
4	$(1 \times 2^2) + (0 \times 2^1) + (0 \times 2^0)$	100
5	$(1 \times 2^2) + (0 \times 2^1) + (1 \times 2^0)$	101

. . . and so on. As the numbers grow larger, their binary translations begin to look unwieldy to our eyes—the number 4096, for instance, expressed in binary terms is 1000000000000—but computers thrive on binary numbers, because they can be expressed by on-off switches, which are among the most exquisitely simple of all mechanical devices. A computer that employed ten-based numbers would have to have ten settings at each of its millions of circuit junctures, plus a storage system with ten possible states at every point, but a binary computer requires only that each

of these millions of switches and encoding points have two
states—0 = off and 1 = on. These states may be represented
by the presence or absence of punch holes, as was done with
the cards and paper tape employed in the 1950s, or of
magnetically charged dots on a disc, as in the floppy discs
and hard discs of the seventies and eighties, or of dark
dots on the optical discs that promise to become the data
storage standard of the nineties. Whatever the medium may
be, it's all bits—zeros and ones, off and on states—to a
computer.

Anything that can be quantified can be digitized, including sound (a compact disc containing nothing but zeros and
ones can reproduce Mozart and Harry Partch), pictures
(bits inscribed on laser discs can replicate Hollywood movies
or paintings in the Louvre), and abstractions ranging from
computer models of rotating galaxies to the EKG patterns
of heart attack victims. It is because binary digits act as
common currency for every quantifiable phenomenon that
an ordinary desktop computer can be applied to an enormous variety of tasks, from calculating bank balances and
designing shoes to flying spacecraft and guiding tunnel-
digging machines under the English Channel. And that is
why scientists, too, whether they are engaged in sequencing
frog DNA or imaging distant quasars, increasingly find that
their time is spent manipulating bits of data.

Information theory is still in its infancy, and has many
shortcomings. One glaring limitation is that *IT* cannot yet
be employed to access the *significance* of a piece of information. Presented with two telegrams dispatched from Tokyo
on September 2, 1945—one reading, "The war is over!" and
the other, "The cat is dead!"—*IT* declares that since the bit
count of each telegram is approximately equal, both contain
about the same amount of information, even though the

first telegram obviously would have meant more to most readers than the second (unless the second message was a code; coding is an important question in information theory, but one that I'll not go into here). By relating information to thermodynamics, *IT* postulates that no system can generate more than the total amount of information put into it; there is, in other words, a law of conservation of information, comparable to the conservation of energy. Fair enough, but if we regard the brain as an information-processing system, the conservation law implies that Beethoven's string quartets, say, contain no more information than the total of everything Beethoven had learned plus the entropy bill paid by the meals he ate and the air he breathed while composing them. This may be true in a way, but it's not very illuminating. Leon Brillouin, a physicist whose writings did much to call attention to the significance of information theory, tried to quantify the way that human creativity seems to reduce the amount of entropy in the subjects it addresses, but his effort was probably premature and in any event it failed. Information theory is hardly alone in this, however; human thought is a dark continent to every science.

Yet even in its infancy, *IT* can contribute to explaining the dialogue between mind and nature. Consider what it has to say about questions concerning the brain, biological systems more generally, and quantum physics.

The human nervous system can be analyzed as a data-processing system, with intriguing results. Much of the current excitement about "neural networks"—artificial-intelligence computer systems set up to model the brain—derives from the fact that neurons in the brain, like microswitches in a computer, have but two fundamental states: At any given time each either fires or does not, and so is in a state equivalent to either 1 or 0. This may provide the *IT* basis for the proof, published by Warren S. McCulloch and Walter Pitts in the 1940s, that the brain is a "Turing machine," meaning that it can do anything a computer can do.

When neurologists inform us that the 125 million photosensitive receptors in the human eye have a total potential data output of over a billion bits per second, and that this exceeds both the carrying capacity of the optic nerve and the data processing rate of the brain's higher cortical centers, we can by using information theory alone hypothesize that the eye must somehow reduce the data it gathers before sending them through the optic nerve to the brain. And, indeed, clinical experiments with human vision indicate that the eye does resort to various data-reduction tricks. To get a sense of just how successful these tactics can be—though this particular deception is relatively trivial— cover your left eye, look at the page number atop the left page of this book, and place a coin near the gutter between the pages. Keeping your right eye fixed on the page number and your left eye covered, move the coin right and left; you will find that there is a spot where the coin *vanishes.* This is the blind spot in the eye. It represents the hole— rather a large hole, actually—where the optic nerve exits through the retina. Note that where the coin disappears you perceive not a black hole but white paper. Yet there is no paper there: The *coin* is there. What the eye is doing, evidently, is filling in the hole with whatever color—in this case, white—surrounds the hole. (Try the experiment on a red sheet of paper, and you will "see" that the blind spot is red.) The fact that the eye must employ some such data-reduction tactics can be predicted by information theory independently of the clinical case studies.

IT offers similar insights into memory. The brain's short-term memory can store only about seven digits in the ten-based system; that's why people have trouble remembering telephone numbers more than seven digits long, and resist efforts by the post office to employ postal zip codes longer than seven digits. *IT* postulates that data overload results not in the loss of just a few extra digits, but in a general corruption of the data in memory. And that's what we experience: When we try to remember a long telephone number we don't normally forget just the last few digits, but are apt to scramble much of the number. Teachers, familiar with the danger of memory overload, take care to explain basic concepts before building on them, lest their students become totally confused and "turn off."

Biological reproduction, too, can be likened to a communications channel, one that has evolved through natural selection to maximize its data capacity and minimize error. The DNA molecule, that basis of all terrestrial life, encodes bits of information in triplets of four chemical substances, the nucleotide bases. (The bases are Adenine, Guanine, Cytosine, and Thymine; their triplets correspond to the twenty primary amino acids from which proteins are built.) DNA molecules use this code to synthesize proteins by employing the appropriate sequence of amino acids. It turns out that the error rate in DNA replication approaches the best that information theory permits; biological evolution can be viewed as an ongoing effort to minimize the amount of "noise" in the DNA-RNA communications channel that transmits genetic data down through the generations.

Before information theory can be incorporated into quantum physics, however, we will need to identify a binary code of some sort in the subatomic world—the equivalent, in all matter and energy, of the two-based numbering system employed by digital computers and by the brain.

Quantum theory implies that this may be possible. The
word *quantum* (from the Greek for "how much") reflects the
fact that matter and energy as we observe them are not
continuous, but present themselves in discrete units, the
quanta. Quantum mechanics can be construed as meaning
that not only matter and energy but *knowledge* is quantized,
in that information about any system can be reduced to a set
of fundamental, irreducible units. Quanta alone, however,
cannot yet provide us with the two-based numbering system
we'd like to have in order to interpret the entire physical
world in terms of bits, because quanta as we currently
understand them have not two but many different states.
An ingredient is missing.

In search of a binary code through which information
theory could be universally applied to physics, the physicist
John Archibald Wheeler looks to yes-or-no choices made by
the observer—like the choice, in the dual slit experiment, of
whether we ask the electron to represent itself as a wave or
a particle. Wheeler suggests that all the concepts we apply to
nature, including the concept of *objects*, may be built up
from on-off decisions made by the scientist in the way he or
she chooses to set up each experimental apparatus. He
encapsulates this dynamic in the slogan "It from bit":

> Every *it*—every particle, every field of force, even the
> spacetime continuum itself—derives its function, its mean-
> ing, its very existence entirely . . . from the apparatus-
> elicited answers to yes or no questions, binary choices, *bits*.

Quantum physics deals with the classically-engendered
paradox of what things "really are" by declining to assign an
identity to any phenomenon *until it has been observed*. As
Wheeler likes to say, paraphrasing Bohr, "No phenomenon
is a phenomenon until it is an *observed* phenomenon."

An observation, in turn, is defined as consisting of two operations. First, we "collapse the wave function." This means that energy (and with it some potential information) is collected, as by intercepting light from a star or X-rays from a high-energy particle collision. Second, there must be an irreversible act of *amplification* that *records* the observational data, as when the starlight darkens silver grains on a photographic plate or the X-rays trigger an electronic detector. The second part of the definition clearly is necessary; otherwise, all the starlight that has ever washed over the lifeless lava planes of the moon could be said to have been observed, which would be to generalize the concept of observation into meaninglessness. But the idea of amplification is also intriguingly open-ended: It implies that for an observation to qualify *as* an observation, the data must not only be recorded but also be *communicated* somehow.

Suppose that an automatic telescope, run by a computer at an unmanned mountaintop observatory, records the light of an exploding star—a supernova—in a distant galaxy. The wave function has been collapsed but not fully amplified, for it has not yet been communicated to an intelligent being.* (To argue otherwise we should have to say that any record of a process constitutes an observation, in which case we would be obliged to contend that every time a cosmic ray etches a path in a moon rock it has been observed, and that seems absurd.) The next morning an astronomer visits the observatory and views on a computer screen the dot etched by the exploding star. *Now* we have an act of observation, no?

Maybe not; here things get strange. Let's say that the astronomer goes to the telephone to call a colleague and tell

---

*It does not matter who makes and communicates the observational data; any sensate being can qualify, whether he or she or it is a Harvard astrophysicist or a silicon network terminal embedded in an asteroid.

her that he has discovered a supernova—but before he can do so an avalanche buries his laboratory, killing him and destroying his data. Has an observation occurred? As there is now no more information about the supernova than there was before the astronomer arrived on the mountaintop (less, in fact) the only correct answer appears to be no! As Wheeler puts it, an observer is "one who operates an observing device *and participates in the making of meaning*" (emphasis added). If the sole observer is dead, no meaning has been adduced. There is no observation without communication—and no observation means no phenomenon in the known universe, which according to the view I have been espousing means no phenomenon, period.

Quantum physics thus confronts us with a nest of Chinese boxes. For any given observation there is a conceptual "box" within which an observation has been made. The wave function is in there, along with the apparatus that amplified it and the intelligent being who participated in giving it meaning. But this box, in turn, is enclosed within an infinite number of larger boxes wherein the news of the event has not yet been received and interpreted. For residents of these larger boxes, the phenomenon has not (yet) occurred.*

Which leads me to a final look at the question of interstellar communications.

Imagine, sad thought, that the sun were to blow up tomorrow, destroying all the world's knowledge, and that no creature intercepted the broadcasts weakly and inadvert-

---

*Chinese boxes show up in classical, macroscopic physics, too, owing to the fact that no information may be transmitted faster than the velocity of light. Suppose that the unstable star Eta Carinae, thousands of light years from Earth, "already" has exploded, and that astronomers on planets near Eta Carinae have photographed the explosion. Nevertheless the explosion has not yet occurred so far as we are concerned, because light from the explosion has not yet reached us. (At least it had not as of 3 hours Greenwich Mean Time on the night of September 11, 1991.)

ently leaked into space by terrestrial radio and television transmitters prior to our planet's demise. This scenario parallels that of the unfortunate astrophysicist buried in the avalanche: No act of observation! All human science, then, would in the long run have added up to nothing. Having made no lasting contribution to science on the panstellar scale, we would have bequeathed nothing to the totality of the perceived universe.

How do we avoid the pointlessness of such a dismal denouement? By contributing what we know to other, alien intelligences—either by sending information to them directly or dispatching it to be stored in an interstellar communications network. *That* act of amplification would insure that our observations were not hostaged to the fate of our one species, but instead had been added to the sum of galactic and intergalactic knowledge, stretching far across space and into the future. As Wheeler writes, "How far foot and ferry have carried meaning-making communication in fifty thousand years gives faint feel for how far interstellar propagation is destined to carry it in fifty billion years."

When speculating about interstellar communication one gets the odd feeling that there is something natural and intuitive about it—that we are *meant* to do it, as we are meant to write poetry, love our children, fret about the future and cherish the past. Perhaps this inchoate connotation of appropriateness, sustaining as it does so many SETI researchers through their long and daunting quest to make contact with life elsewhere among the stars, derives from this: That by participating in interstellar communication we would not just be exchanging facts and opinions and art and entertainment, but would be adding to the total of cosmic understanding. If we have companions in the universe, then the cosmic tree is not rooted in earthly soil alone. Wherever there is life and thought the roots may thrive, until in their grand and growing extent they begin to match the glory of the tree's starry crown.

Why, then, are a lonely few astronomers hunched over the consoles of the radio telescopes, forever listening, seeking, hoping? Perhaps because in some sense we suspect that the known universe is being built out there, in countless minds, and that we can help it flourish. We who came down from out of the forest seek to grow a forest of knowing among the stars.

Notes

PREFACE

Page xi

"All things without . . ." The lines by Sir John Davies come from his poem *Nosce Teipsum;* I have taken the liberty of modernizing his spelling and punctuation.

"Living matter and clarity are opposites." Max Born, *The Born-Einstein Letters* (New York: Walker, 1971), p. 95.

THIS IS NOT THE UNIVERSE

Page 3

"The mind does not understand its own reason for being." In Suzi Gablik, "A Conversation with René Magritte," *Studio International*, vol. 173, no. 887 (March 1967), p. 128; in René Magritte, *Secret Affinities* (Houston: Institute for the Arts, Rice University, 1976), p. 9.

"A picture without a frame is not a picture." In Dennis Overbye, *Lonely Hearts of the Cosmos: The Story of the Scientific Quest for the Secret of the Universe* (New York: Harper Collins, 1991), galley proof p. 108.

Page 7

"The world is a fantasy . . ." Dennis Sciama, interview with TF, Padua, Italy, July 1983.

The first mention of the word "scientist" listed in the *Oxford English Dictionary* was by the philosopher and mathematician William Whewell, who wrote in 1840, "We need very much a name to describe a cultivator of science in general. I should incline to call him a scientist."

Page 9

"The scientist asks not what are the currently most important questions . . ." Ludwig Boltzmann, *Theoretical Physics and Philosophical Problems,* ed. Brian McGuinness (Boston: D. Reidel, 1974), p. 14.

Page 10

"But all the more splendid . . ." Ludwig Boltzmann, *Theoretical Physics and Philosophical Problems,* ed. Brian McGuinness (Boston: D. Reidel, 1974), p. 14

Page 12

Here is a solution to the nine-dots puzzle:

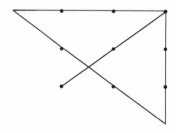

Page 12

". . . the infinite universe." We do not yet know whether the geometry of the universe is open, in which case the universe is spatially infinite, or closed, in which case it is finite. But in either case the observable universe is infinite in the sense that it contains an inexhaustible amount of information.

Page 15

"Science cannot solve the ultimate mystery of Nature . . ." In John D. Barrow and Frank R. Tipler, *The Anthropic Cosmological Principle* (New York: Oxford University Press, 1986), galley proof p. 110.

"When I look at my work I think I'm in the heart of mystery . . ." In René Magritte, *Secret Affinities* (Houston: Institute for the Arts, Rice University, 1976), p. 9.

"The feeling we experience . . ." In René Magritte, *Secret Affinities* (Houston: Institute for the Arts, Rice University, 1976), p. 7.

"The vision of the universe that is so vivid in our minds . . ." John Archibald Wheeler, "Law Without Law," in John Archibald Wheeler and Wojciech Hubert Zurek, eds., *Quantum Theory and Measurement* (Princeton, N.J.: Princeton University Press, 1983), unpaginated manuscript.

THE ENORMOUS RADIO

Page 17

I've borrowed the title of this chapter from that of a short story by John Cheever. See his *The Enormous Radio, and Other Stories* (New York: Funk & Wagnalls, 1953).

"Maybe we're here only to say . . ." Rainer Maria Rilke, *Duino Elegies*, Ninth Elegy, trans. A. Poulin, Jr. (Boston: Houghton Mifflin, 1977), p. 63.

"Flout 'em and scout 'em . . ." William Shakespeare, *The Tempest*, III, ii, 118.

Page 19

"It would be strange . . ." In F.M. Cornford, "Innumerable Worlds in Presocratic Philosophy," *The Classical Quarterly* (January 1934), p. 13.

"Upon one tree there are many fruits . . ." Joseph Needham, trans., in *SETI: Search for Extraterrestrial Intelligence* (Washington: NASA NP-114, 1990), p. 3.

Page 21

". . . conclusive evidence of these crafty critters can be found at checkout counters from coast to coast." Rep. Silvio Conte, *Congressional Record*, June 23, 1990, H4356.

Page 22

". . . a signature of civilization." One of the problems confronting any SETI project is that we don't know at what radio frequency an alien civilization might choose to transmit. And even if we did know, the received frequency would be altered ("Doppler shifted") by the drift of the sun and the alien's home star through space, and by the velocities of the planets in their orbits around those stars. So the preferred approach is to listen to many frequencies simultaneously, relying on computers to sound the alarm if they spot a signal.

Page 22

". . . beaming greetings our way." Suppose, for the sake of argument, that fully *ten thousand* beacons were sending radio signals that we could detect, and we managed to tune our receivers to the correct frequency to receive them. If there are one hundred billion (10^{11}) stars in our galaxy, then the odds that any given star will be the site of one of the ten thousand transmitting worlds is 10^{11} divided by 10,000, or one in ten million. We would have to search half this number, or five million, stars to have a 50/50 chance of acquiring the signal. Even if we used a superlatively efficient radio telescope—one that could examine a star every hour, twenty-four hours a day—it would take about sixty years to observe five million stars. An all-sky search reduces the search time dramatically, but at the cost of lower sensitivity. Since we don't know how powerful a signal might be, the best strategy is probably the one being adopted by NASA—to run all-sky and star-by-star searches simultaneously.

Page 24

"The one thing that has consistently improved survival value has been intelligence. . . . " In Timothy Ferris, "An End to Cosmic Loneliness," *The New York Times Magazine*, October 23, 1977, p. 99.

Page 24

"The adaptive value of intelligence . . ." Carl Sagan and I. S. Shklovskii, *Intelligent Life in the Universe* (New York: Dell, 1966), p. 411.

". . . our neuroanatomy almost certainly has been duplicated nowhere else in the universe." Neither would we expect our gross anatomy to be duplicated elsewhere. As the American naturalist Loren Eiseley wrote in 1937, "Life, even cellular life, may exist out yonder in the dark. But high or low in nature, it will not wear the shape of man. That shape is the evolutionary product of a strange, long wandering through the attics of the forest roof, and so great are the chances of failure, that nothing precisely and identically human is likely ever to come that way again." Loren Eiseley, *The Immense Journey* (New York: Random House, 1937), quoted in Nicholas Rescher, "Extraterrestrial Science," in Edward Regis, ed. *Extraterrestrials: Science and Alien Intelligence* (Cambridge, England: Cambridge University Press, 1985), p. 113.

Page 26

". . . the adventurer William Strachey." Strachey's account is reproduced in Louis B. Wright, ed., *A Voyage to Virginia in 1609: Two Narratives, Strachey's "True Reportory" and Jourdain's "Discovery of the Bermudas"* . . . , (Charlottesville: University Press of Virginia, 1964).

Page 27

". . . When thou camest first / Thou did strok'st me . . ." William Shakespeare, *The Tempest*, I, ii, 333ff.

Page 28

"The vault of heaven . . ." Fyodor Dostoyevsky, *The Brothers Karamazov*, trans. Constance Garnett (New York: Modern Library), p. 380.

Page 29

"The probability of success is difficult to estimate . . ." Giuseppe Cocconi and Philip Morrison, "Searching for Interstellar Communications," *Nature* (September 19, 1959).

THE CENTRAL NERVOUS SYSTEM OF THE MILKY WAY GALAXY

Page 31

"I have loved my fellow men . . ." Quoted in Lawrence LeShan and Jerry Margenau, *Einstein's Space and Van Gogh's Sky* (New York: Macmillan, 1982), p. 141.

"Heaven and earth shall pass away . . ." Bible, King James translation, Matthew 24:35.

Page 35

". . . to establish an interstellar network." I originally proposed the feasibility of interstellar networks in an article, "The Universe as an Ocean of Thought," published in *Harper's* magazine in July 1975.

Page 36

"Much has been written . . ." For a discussion of self-replicating probes as an argument against the existence of extraterrestrial intelligence, see John D. Barrow and Frank Tipler, *The Anthropic Cosmological Principle* (Oxford University Press, 1986), chapter 9. Barrow and Tipler estimate the cost of launching the first slow-speed probe as of order only a few tens of billions of dollars; all the subsequent probes are free, in that they are replicated by the original probe and its descendants without cost to the originating society.

Page 36

"The original probe would be small. . . ." Interestingly, while the probe's antenna, propulsion engine, meteor shield, etc., might have to be relatively large—we don't really know much about the technology of interstellar spacecraft—its high-capacity memory banks evidently could be tiny. A study of the theoretical limits of memory storage conducted by Richard Feynman indicates that all the information in all Earth's libraries could be stored in a sphere smaller than the period at the end of this sentence.

Page 40

". . . a computer 'as intelligent' as a human . . ." For a searching if rather exotic argument against the proposition that machines can think like people, see Roger Penrose, *The Emperor's New Mind: Concerning Computers, Minds, and the Laws of Physics* (New York: Oxford University Press, 1990).

". . . memory plus perception is the basis of intelligence . . ." For discussions of the vital role played by memory in human intelligence see, e.g., a paper by the Italian psychoanalyst Eugenio Gaddini, "Notes on the Mind-Body Question," *International Journal of Psycho-Analysis*, 68(3), (1987), p. 316, in which he argues that memory plays "a crucial role in the passage from physiological to mental functioning." See also Gerald M. Edelman, *The Remembered Present: A Biological Theory of Consciousness* (New York: Basic Books, 1989), and George Johnson, *In the Palaces of Memory* (New York: Knopf, 1991).

Page 44

"This is as strange a maze . . ." William Shakespeare, *The Tempest*, V, i, 242ff.

"A great while ago the world begun . . ." William Shakespeare, *Twelfth Night*, V, i, 393ff.

BEING THERE

Page 45

"We may begin to see reality differently . . ." Heinz Pagels, *The Dreams of Reason: The Computer and the Rise of the Sciences of Complexity* (New York: Simon & Schuster, 1988), p. 13.

Page 51

". . . Simon's shoe repair shop." VR may offer a way of ameliorating the data glut that currently afflicts many fields of science. Evidence of the ozone hole over Antarctica, for instance, languished unexamined in data tapes for years before experts got round to reducing the data that revealed it; had the tapes been made available in the form of VR simulations of the earth, even a child could have noticed the ozone hole. Indeed, this is one of the exciting educational prospects for VR; high school science students searching through depictions of recent data received from space and downloaded by satellite to their school computers might have a genuine chance of making important discoveries before the professional scientists did.

DOG'S LIFE

Page 59

"I am the dog . . ." William Shakespeare, *The Two Gentlemen of Verona*, II, iii, 20ff.

"Dog? To be dog?" Leon Rooke, *Shakespeare's Dog* (New York: Knopf, 1983), p. 6.

Page 60

"Dogs are very loyal." In Reinhold Bergler, *Man and Dog: The Psychology of a Relationship*, trans. Brian Rasmussen and Dana Loewy (Boston: Blackwell, 1988), pp. 95, 100.

". . . dogs alone have elected subservience to man." I realize that this may sound a bit harsh, given that the early stages of their domestication must have involved beatings and other exertions of force against wild dogs. Also involved, however, was a degree of self-selection: The wild dogs that were willing to venture into human habitats, e.g., to beg for food, were the ones most often captured and domesticated. Incidentally, all varieties of *Canis familiaris* hunt in packs, and their devotion to a human master is thought to derive from their innate reliance on a pack leader.

"He leapt on them and killed them both . . ." Muhammad ibn Khalaf Ibn al-Marzuban, *The Book of the Superiority of*

Dogs Over Many of Those Who Wear Clothes, translated and edited by G.R. Smith and M.A.S. Abdel Haleem (Warminster, England: Aris and Phillips, 1978), p. 30.

Page 61

"I am fine dog." Rudyard Kipling, "Thy Servant a Dog," in his *Collected Dog Stories* (London: Macmillan, 1934), p. 163.

Page 62

"The person who has cancer . . ." In Richard Berendzen, ed., *Life Beyond Earth & the Mind of Man* (Washington, D.C.: NASA, 1973), p. 49.

"We might hear from near-immortals . . ." Philip Morrison, ed., *SETI: The Search for Extraterrestrial Intelligence* (Mountain View, California: NASA Ames Research Center, 1976), p. 8.

". . . a useful and character-building experience . . ." In Richard Berendzen, ed., *Life Beyond Earth & the Mind of Man* (Washington, D.C.: NASA, 1973), p. 64.

Page 65

"How do dogs feel about your God, Krister?" In Richard Berendzen, ed., *Life Beyond Earth & the Mind of Man* (Washington, D.C.: NASA, 1973), pp. 59, 60.

"You might even have to reorganize your behavior to dogs . . ." In Richard Berendzen, ed., *Life Beyond Earth & the Mind of Man* (Washington, D.C.: NASA, 1973), p. 70.

THE INTERPRETER

Page 71

"As long as the brain is a mystery . . ." In Victor Cohn, "Charting 'the Soul's Frail Dwelling-House,'" *The Washington Post*, September 5, 1982, Final Edition, p. A1.

"One of the most misleading techniques . . ." Ludwig Wittgenstein, *Philosophical Remarks*, ed. Rush Rhees, trans. Raymond Hargreaves and Roger White (Chicago: University of Chicago Press, 1975), p. 88.

Page 72

"The strong subjective sense . . ." Michael S. Gazzaniga, *The Social Brain* (New York: Basic Books, 1985), p. 189.

Page 73

"The mother of invention . . ." In Judith Hooper and Dick Teresi, *The Three-Pound Universe* (New York: Dell, 1986), p. 43.

Page 74

". . . experiments . . . conducted by Benjamin Libet . . ." Earlier research in areas related to Libet's was carried out by Wilder Penfield, by Sir John Eccles, and by Robert Porter and Corbie Brinkman. Also relevant was the work of Nils Lassen and Per Roland in Copenhagen.

Page 75

"Their neurons were firing a third of a second before they were even conscious of the desire to act . . ." In Tom Siegfried, "How Free Is Free Will?" *The Miami Herald*, March 5, 1989, p. 10G.

Page 78

"Going to get a Coke." Michael S. Gazzaniga, *The Social Brain* (New York: Basic Books, 1985), p. 72.

"The patient always gives some more or less adequate reason for doing what he does." John R. Searle, *Minds, Brains, and Science* (London: British Broadcasting Corp., 1984), p. 90.

Page 79

"I want to learn about French food . . ." Michael S. Gazzaniga, *The Social Brain* (New York: Basic Books, 1985), p. 5.

Page 80

"Language is merely the press agent . . ." In Judith Hooper and Dick Teresi, *The Three-Pound Universe* (New York: Dell, 1986), p. 235.

THE UNITY OF THE UNIVERSE AND OF THE HUMAN MIND

Page 83

"All things are one." In G.S. Kirk, *Heraclitus the Cosmic Fragments* (Cambridge University Press, 1962), p. 65.

"Nature tools along . . ." Allan Sandage, telephone conversation with TF, January 1990.

Page 85

"I experienced a rocking sensation . . ." Gopi Krishna, *Kundalini* (London: Robinson & Watkins, 1971), pp. 12–13.

"Who am I, that I should go unto Pharaoh . . ." Bible, King James translation, Exodus 3:11.

Page 86

"I have felt / A presence . . ." William Wordsworth, *Poetical Works, Seven Volumes in Three* (Boston: Hurd & Houghton, 1877), vol. II, 198:189; quoted in Richard Maurice Bucke, *Cosmic Consciousness* (New York: Dutton, 1969), p. 286.

"The everlasting and triumphant mystical tradition . . ." William James, *The Varieties of Religious Experience* (New York: Modern Library), p. 140.

Pages 87–88

"There was a sound like a nerve thread snapping . . ." Gopi Krishna, *Kundalini* (London: Robinson & Watkins, 1971), p. 66.

Page 88

"Conviction . . . ineffability . . . unity." I am drawing here primarily on studies by the American philosopher William James, the English physician and author Richard Maurice Bucke, the Zen scholar D.T. Suzuki, and the American professor of philosophy W.T. Stace.

Pages 88–89

"Any enlightenment which requires to be authenticated is false . . ." Reginald Blyth, *Zen and Zen Classics* (Tokyo: Hokusiedo, 1964), vol. 2, p. 37.

Page 89

"The life of this world is but a play and a sport." The Koran, Part II, trans. E.H. Palmer; in Richard Maurice Bucke, *Cosmic Consciousness* (New York: Dutton, 1969), p. 129.

"The five colors blind the eye . . ." Lao Tzu, *Tao te Ching*, trans. Gia-fu Feng and Jane English (New York: Knopf, 1974) Chapter 12.

"This life's five windows . . ." In Lawrence LeShan and Jerry Margenau, *Einstein's Space and Van Gogh's Sky* (New York: Macmillan Publishing Co., 1982), p. 249.

"It can neither be spoken nor written about . . ." In *The Essential Plotinus*, trans. Elmer O'Brien (Indianapolis: Hackett, 1984), p. 78.

"The vision baffles telling . . ." In W.T. Stace, *Mysticism and Philosophy* (Los Angeles: Tarcher, 1960), P. 277.

"It is impossible to describe . . ." Gopi Krishna, *Kundalini* (London: Robinson & Watkins, 1971), pp. 12–13.

Page 89

". . . The name that can be named . . ." Lao Tzu, *Tao te Ching*, Chapter 1, TF retranslation.

Page 90

"I should not have left a line to survive me . . ." Plotinus to Flaccus, in Robert Alfred Vaughan, *Hours With the Mystics*, sixth edition (New York: Scribner's, 1893), vol. 1, pp. 78–81.

"The more we say, the more we wish we hadn't . . ." Reginald Blyth, *Zen and Zen Classics* (Tokyo: Hokuseido, 1970), vol. 3, p. 96.

Page 91

"MADAM, WISE MEN NEVER TELL." In Frederick Albert Lang, *The History of Materialism* (London: Kegan Paul, 1925), pp. 324–25.

"Absolute knowledge . . ." Plotinus to Flaccus, in Robert Alfred Vaughan, *Hours With the Mystics*, sixth edition (New York: Scribner's, 1893), vol. 1, pp. 78–81; Plotinus, *Enneads*, VI, 9, in Elmer O'Brien, ed. and trans., *The Essential Plotinus* (Indianapolis: Hackett, 1984), p. 78.

"In mystic states we become one with the Absolute . . ." William James, *The Varieties of Religious Experience* (New York: Modern Library, 1936), p. 140.

"Everything is made of one hidden stuff . . ." Ralph Waldo Emerson, "Self-Reliance," in *Ralph Waldo Emerson, Essays & Lectures*, ed. Joel Porte (New York: Library of America, 1990), pp. 259ff.

Page 91

"The One begets all things." In Elmer O'Brien, ed. and trans., *The Essential Plotinus* (Indianapolis: Hackett, 1984), p. 77.

"The Tao begot one . . ." Lao Tzu, *Tao te Ching*, trans. Gia-fu Feng and Jane English (New York: Knopf, 1974), chapter 42.

"He showed me a little thing . . ." In R.H. Blyth, *Zen and Zen Classics* (Tokyo: Hokusiedo, 1964), vol. 2, p. 47; for a more literal translation see Julian of Norwich, *Revelations of Divine Love*, trans. Clifton Wolters (London: Penguin, 1966), p. 68.

Page 92

"In a grain of dust are all the scrolls . . ." In Heinrich Dumoulin, *Zen Enlightenment: Origins and Meaning* (New York: Weatherhill, 1979), p. 104.

"There are things that are so serious you can only joke about them." In Ruth Moore, *Niels Bohr* (Cambridge, Massachusetts: MIT Press, 1985), p. 147.

"What is the reflector and what the reflected?" Werner Heisenberg, *Across the Frontiers*, trans. Peter Heath (New York: Harper, 1974), p. 34.

"The most beautiful emotion we can experience is the mystical . . ." Albert Einstein, *The World as I See It* (New York: Philosophical Library, 1934); in Philipp Frank, *Einstein: His Life and Times* (New York: Knopf, 1970), p. 284.

Page 93

"God of Abraham, God of Isaac . . ." In Evelyn Underhill, *Mysticism: A Study in the Nature and Development of Man's Spiritual Consciousness* (New York: Dutton, 1961), p. 189.

". . . grandeur of the human soul." In Francis X.J. Coleman, *Neither Angel Nor Beast: The Life and Work of Blaise Pascal* (New York: Routledge & Kegan Paul, 1986), p. 61.

Page 94

"The thrice-great Hermes." Copernicus, *On the Revolutions*, trans. Charles Glenn Wallis (Chicago: University of Chicago Press, 1952), pp. 526–27.

"A vital agent diffused through everything . . ." In Richard S. Westfall, *Never At Rest: A Biography of Isaac Newton* (Cambridge: Cambridge University Press, 1980), p. 304.

Page 96

"Satori may be defined . . ." D.T. Suzuki, *Essays in Zen Buddhism: First Series* (New York: Grove Press, 1978), p. 230.

JOE MONTANA'S PREMOTOR CORTEX

Page 100

". . . there are many sorts of intelligence." For an analysis of the multiple-intelligence view of the brain, see Howard Gardner, *Frames of Mind: The Theory of Multiple Intelligences* (New York: Basic Books, 1985).

Page 101

"Everything looked easy." Robert Oates, Jr., "Mind Over Matter," *Don Heinrich's Pro Preview* (Seattle, Washington: Preview Publishing, 1990), p. 8.

Page 104

"I'm going to take a nice nap." In Mark Heisler, "Comfy Joe Could Have Won This From Easy Chair," *Los Angeles Times*, January 29, 1990, part C, p. 3.

"Football's Fred Astaire." In *The New York Times*, January 22, 1990.

Pages 104–5

"I seestepthrow." In Irvin Muchnick, "Joe Montana: The State of the Art," *The New York Times Magazine*, December 17, 1989, p. 61.

Page 105

"It might screw up the whole process." In Joe Montana and Bob Raissman, *Audibles: My Life in Football* (New York: Morrow, 1986), p. 64.

Page 106

"It's like a movie running through my mind." In Joe Montana and Bob Raissman, *Audibles: My Life in Football* (New York: Morrow, 1986), p. 141.

"You've got to mentally dominate the game . . ." Harry Edwards, interview with TF, Berkeley, February 26, 1990.

Page 107

"For a quarterback the game is at least seventy per cent mental." Joe Montana and Bob Raissman, *Audibles: My Life in Football* (New York: Morrow, 1986), p. 141.

Page 108

". . . cortex grows in size." For a review of the surprising finding that cortical maps change in response to behavior rather than being fixed from birth, see J.T. Wall, "Variable Organization in Cortical Maps . . ." *Trends in Neurosciences*, vol. 11 (1988), pp. 549–57.

Page 110

"The supposed specialization of the left brain for language . . ." William H. Calvin, "Bootstrapping Thought; Is Consciousness a Darwinian Sidestep," Reality Club lecture, *Whole Earth Review* (June 22, 1987), p. 22.

Page 111

"If I can make a mechanical model I can understand it . . ." In P.N. Johnson-Laird, "The Ghost-Hunters," *Times Literary Supplement*, December 14, 1984, p. 1441.

"The proper method for inquiring after the properties of things is to deduce them from experiments." In Richard S. Westfall, *Never At Rest: A Biography of Isaac Newton* (Cambridge University Press, 1980), p. 248.

Page 112

"Nothing is 'mere.'" Richard Feynman, *The Feynman Lectures of Physics* (Reading, Mass.: Addison-Wesley, 1963), vol. 1, p. 3–6.

Page 113

"What computers can't do very well is to *act*." For more on robot shortcomings, see Greg Freiherr, "Invasion of the Spacebots," *Air & Space* (February/March 1990), pp. 73ff.

". . . the intellectual acme of human thought." Hans Moravec, *Mind Children: The Future of Robot and Human Intelligence* (Cambridge: Harvard University Press, 1988), p. 16.

Page 114

"'How can the shot be loosed if "I" do not do it?'" E. Herrigel, *Zen in the Art of Archery* (London: Routledge, 1953), pp. 73–74.

Page 115

"He recently put together a tape recorder . . ." In R.M. Restak, "Islands of Genius," *Science 82* (May, 1982), p. 63.

BELLY LAUGHS

Page 117

"Progress is nothing but the victory of laughter over dogma." In Edmund Bergler, *Laughter and the Sense of Humor* (New York: Intercontinental, 1956), p. xii.

"Comedy is a serious business." In Tom Dardis, *Keaton: The Man Who Wouldn't Lie Down* (New York: Limelight Editions, 1979), p. 131.

Page 118

"Every laugh is a paradox." Heartfelt laughter is essentially involuntary, though we can to some degree control it, as we can other involuntary spasms such as coughing. The English physician and humorist Jonathan Miller notes that when a stroke victim who has lost control of the muscles on one side of his face is *asked* to grin, "they respond by grinning on just one side." But when the same patient encounters something amusing, he breaks into a grin that animates *both* sides of the face. See John Durant and Jonathan Miller, eds., *Laughing Matters: A Serious Look at Humor* (London: Longman, 1988), p. 8.

"Laughter has no greater foe than emotion." In Wylie Sypher, ed., *Comedy: George Meredith, "An Essay on Comedy," and Henri Bergson, "Laughter"* (Baltimore: Johns Hopkins University Press, 1980, 1956), pp. 63–64.

"The human child 'lacks all feeling for the comic.'" In Max Eastman, *Enjoyment of Laughter* (New York: Simon and Schuster, 1937), p. 36.

Page 119

". . . Norman Cousins engineered his recovery . . ." For an account of his recovery see Norman Cousins, *Anatomy of an Illness as Perceived by the Patient* (New York: Bantam, 1981), p. 39.

"A fool lifteth up his voice with laughter . . ." Bible, King James translation, Ecclesiastes xxi, 20. In I Corinthians 3:18, however, we find the assertion that "if any man [thinks he is] wise in this world, let him become a fool, that he may [really] be wise."

"Loud laughter is the mirth of the mob . . ." Lord Chesterfield, letter to his son, October 19, 1748.

". . . Cervantes . . ." "I have heard that a great poet of antiquity once said that it was a difficult thing not to write satire," says Cipión in Miguel de Cervantes' "The Dialogue of the Dogs," from his *Six Exemplary Novels,* trans. Harriet de Onís (Woodbury, N.Y.: Barron's, 1961), p. 8.

Page 122

"Spasmodic contractions . . ." Norman N. Holland, *Laughing: A Psychology of Humor* (Ithaca, New York: Cornell University Press, 1982), p. 76.

"Apt to burst into loud laughter . . ." In Edmund Bergler, *Laughter and the Sense of Humor* (New York: Intercontinental, 1956), p. 17.

Page 123

"Life is too serious . . ." In Tom Dardis, *Keaton: The Man Who Wouldn't Lie Down* (New York: Limelight Editions, 1979), p. 198.

Page 123

"He is aware of death at every moment . . ." In Robert Payne, *The Great God Pan: A Biography of the Tramp Played by Charles Chaplin* (New York: Hermitage House, 1952), p. 20.

Page 125

"See it? I *directed* it." *The Jack Benny Show,* written by Sam Perrin, George Balzer, Al Gordon, and Hal Goldman, untitled episode broadcast December 1, 1957, UCLA Research Library Special Collections 134, box 46, folio 3, script p. 18.

"I'm *thinking it over!*" In Irving A. Fein, *Jack Benny: An Intimate Biography* (New York: Putnam's, 1976), p. 144.

". . . paradox, the ultimate incongruity." A young boy said to his father: "Father, I want to marry granny." His father laughed at him and said, "You can't marry my mother." The boy replied, "Why not? You married mine." Paradoxes of this sort are found in all languages, even mathematics.

Page 127

Chaplin "had a way of kicking people . . ." In Robert Payne, *The Great God Pan: A Biography of the Tramp Played by Charles Chaplin* (New York: Hermitage House, 1952), p. 84.

Page 128

"I could not even whimper." In Tom Dardis, *Keaton: The Man Who Wouldn't Lie Down* (New York: Limelight Editions, 1979), p. 11.

Page 128

"Jests which slap the face are not good jests." In Max Eastman, *Enjoyment of Laughter* (New York: Simon and Schuster, 1937), p. 330.

"Laughter is an affection . . ." Immanuel Kant, *Critique of Judgment*, trans. Bernard, pp. 220–225; in Ralph Piddington, *The Psychology of Laughter* (New York: Gamut Press, 1963), p. 168.

Page 129

"The cause of laughter . . ." Arthur Schopenhauer, *The World as Will and Idea*, trans. R.B. Haldane and J. Kemp (London: Kegan Paul, 1896), vol. I, p. 76, vol. II, p. 271.

Page 130

"The more a man is capable of entire seriousness . . ." Arthur Schopenhauer, *The World as Will and Idea*, trans. R.B. Haldane and J. Kemp (London: Kegan Paul, 1896), vol. I, p. 76, vol. II, p. 281.

"In humor the little is made great and the great little . . ." In Norman N. Holland, *Laughing: A Psychology of Humor* (Ithaca, New York: Cornell University Press, 1982), p. 101.

"The Great Matter . . . is like the funeral of one's parents . . ." In R.H. Blyth, *Zen and Zen Classics* (Tokyo: Hokuseido Press, 1970), vol. 3, p. 141.

Page 132

"At this Tokusan was enlightened." In R.H. Blyth, *Zen and Zen Classics* (Tokyo: Hokuseido Press, 1974), vol. 4, p. 199.

Page 133

"The gigantic adult menaces the child . . ." The English essayist William Hazlitt pointed out, years ago, that an infant will laugh if an adult first presents him with a threat and then dissipates it: "If we hold a mask before our face, and approach a child with this disguise on, it will at first, from the oddity and incongruity of the appearance, be inclined to laugh; if we go nearer it, steadily, and without saying a word, it will begin to be alarmed, and half inclined to cry; if we suddenly take off the mask, it will recover from its fears, and burst out a-laughing; but if, instead of presenting the old well-known countenance, we have concealed a satyr's head or some frightful caricature behind the first mask, the suddenness of the change will not in this case be a source of merriment to it, but will convert its surprise into an agony of consternation, and will make it scream for help, even though it may be convinced that the whole is a trick at bottom." René Spitz, who beginning in the 1940s studied children's grins and laughter in response to masks, found that infants like to see a smile, but respond even more happily when confronted "by extreme widening of the mouth, somewhat after the manner of a savage animal baring its fangs." See William Hazlitt, "On Wit and Humour," in Geoffrey Keynes, ed. *Selected Essays of William Hazlitt* (New York: Random House, 1934), pp. 411–12; also Edmund Bergler, *Laughter and the Sense of Humor* (New York: Intercontinental, 1956), pp. 11, 57.

DEATH TRIP

Page 135

"It is very beautiful over there . . ." In Ronald Siegel, "The Psychology of Life After Death," *American Psychologist*, 35:10 (October 1980), p. 911.

"This is eternal bliss . . ." Carl Jung, *Memories, Dreams, Reflections*, ed. Aniela Jaffe (New York: Pantheon, 1961), pp. 289–98; in Russell Noyes, Jr., "Dying and Mystical Consciousness," *Journal of Thanatology*, 1:1 (January–February 1971), p. 26.

". . . being in an ecstatic state . . ." In Carol Zaleski, *Otherworld Journeys: Accounts of Near-Death Experience in Medieval and Modern Times* (New York: Oxford University Press, 1987), p. 159.

Pages 135–36

"A sense of profound peace . . ." In Sharon L. Bass, "You Never Recover Your Original Self," *The New York Times*, August 28, 1988, Late City Final Edition, p. 3.

Page 136

"Why did you bring me back?" In Karlis Osis and Erlendur Haraldsson, *At the Hour of Death* (New York: Avon, 1977), p. 4; quoted in Carol Zaleski, *Otherworld Journeys: Accounts of Near-Death Experience in Medieval and Modern Times* (New York: Oxford University Press, 1987), p. 137.

". . . a poor Essex farmer . . ." Thurkill's journey is described in Carol Zaleski, *Otherworld Journeys*, p. 41; see also Nicholas Lehmann in *The Atlantic*, July 1987, p. 96.

Page 136

". . . intense feelings of joy, love, and peace." Raymond A. Moody, *Life After Life* (Harrisburg, Pa.: Stackpole, 1976), pp. 21–22.

Page 137

"How rarely the act of dying appears to be painful . . ." William Osler, *Can. Med. Surg. J.*, 16:511, 1888; in Russell Noyes, Jr., "The Art of Dying," *Perspectives in Biology and Medicine*, vol. 14, No. 3 (Spring 1971), p. 442.

Page 138

"There was no anxiety . . ." Albert Heim, "Remarks on Fatal Falls," 1892, translated in Russell Noyes and Roy Kletti, "The Experience of Dying From Falls," *Omega*, vol. 3 (1972), pp. 45ff.

Page 139

"We are no closer . . ." Raymond A. Moody, *The Light Beyond* (New York: Bantam, 1989), p. 1.

Page 141

". . . there is such a thing as a will to live . . ." Interview on National Public Radio's *All Things Considered*, April 11, 1990.

Page 142

"Among its ministers . . ." In John Dart, "After 'Near-Death,' Atheist Yields Slightly on Afterlife," *Los Angeles Times,* October 8, 1988, Home Edition, part 2, p. 7.

"In cold terror I fell into the abyss . . ." Heinz Pagels, *The Cosmic Code* (New York: Bantam, 1982), p. 349.

Page 143

". . . I will choose the death by which I leave life . . ." In Russell Noyes, Jr., "The Art of Dying," *Perspectives in Biology and Medicine* (Spring, 1971), p. 434.

"My coffin will be Heaven and Earth . . ." Quoted in R.H. Blyth, *Zen and Zen Classics* (Tokyo: Hokuseido Press, 1964), vol. 2, p. 170.

"I sang to the beauty of the stars . . ." Heinz Pagels, *The Cosmic Code* (New York: Bantam, 1982), p. 349.

"Nothing to fear from God . . ." In Giorgio Santillana, *The Origins of Scientific Thought* (New York: New American Library, 1970), p. 289.

Page 144

". . . you would need some mechanism that made dying and death acceptable." Lewis Thomas, interview with TF, New York City, October 20, 1979.

"I could not think of a better way to manage . . . " Lewis Thomas, *The Medusa and the Snail* (New York: Viking, 1979), p. 105.

Page 145

". . . selected on aesthetic grounds . . ." For more on the possibility of aesthetic selection, see Timothy Ferris, *Space-Shots* (New York: Pantheon Books, 1984), introduction.

THINGS THAT GO BUMP

Page 149

"Name now our names . . ." Dennis Tedlock, trans. *Popol Vuh: The Mayan Book of the Dawn of Life* (New York: Simon & Schuster, 1985), p. 78.

"Thunderbolt steers all things." In G. S. Kirk, *Heraclitus the Cosmic Fragments* (Cambridge: Cambridge University Press, 1962), p. 349.

Page 150

"Mark how it mounts, to Man's imperial race . . ." Alexander Pope, *Essay on Man,* Epistle I, VII.

". . . unforeseeable, large-scale changes . . ." For a discussion of possible mechanisms by which the ice ages may have driven *homo* evolution toward higher intelligence, see William H. Calvin, *The Ascent of Mind* (New York: Bantam, 1991).

Page 151

"No cataclysm has desolated the whole world . . ." Charles Darwin, *The Origin of Species by Means of Natural Selection,* sixth edition, 1872 (New York: Modern Library, 1936), p. 373.

Page 152

"Internalization of a tragic metaphor . . ." Robert Reinhold, "California Struggles With The Other Side of Its Dream," *The New York Times,* Sunday, Oct. 22, 1989, 4:1.

Page 155

"A comet nucleus six miles in diameter . . ." The impact of a ten-kilometer diameter object at a velocity of twenty kilometers per second would release approximately seventy million megatons, which is a thousand times the total power of Soviet and American nuclear weapons combined.

Page 158

"Evidence continued to mount . . ." Estimates vary widely as to just how many mass dieouts have occurred, ranging from just five up to two hundred thousand. The fossil record is difficult to read—one is, after all, trying to extract hard data from dirt—and even were the data perfectly reliable, their statistical interpretation would continue to present problems. Amplitude is problematical: All may agree that a dieout has occurred when ninety percent of species perish, but it is more perplexing to determine whether a rise of, say, five percent in the extinction rate constitutes a dieout. Troublesome, too, is the question of periodicity; where some see regular cycles, others see random intervals. For the sake of clarity and coherency I am presenting a case for the new catastrophism that minimizes these uncertainties, on the assumption that the theory will in the long run hold up. This is to some degree a judgment call on my part, and a fully objective account would be rather less assured.

Page 159

Owing to imperfections in the fossil record, the demise of the dinosaurs *might* have taken less than the millions of years usually cited. The paleontologist J. John Sepkoski asserts that "the data (as I and some others read them) are equally consistent with one bad weekend." Private correspondence, March 11, 1991.

". . . tugs at the cloud and perturbs their orbits." This comet shower scenario relies heavily on computer simulations and other studies by Piet Hut of Princeton, Eugene M. Shoemaker of the U.S. Geological Survey in Flagstaff, Arizona, and Paul R. Weissman of the Jet Propulsion Laboratory. See, e.g., Alvarez Hut, et al., "Comet Showers as a Cause of Mass Extinctions," *Nature,* 329:6135 (10 Sept. 1987), pp. 118–26. Also P.R. Weissman, in R.L. Duncombe, ed., *Dynamics of the Solar System* (Dordrecht: Reidel, 1979), pp. 277–82.

Page 162

"The implications of periodicity are profound . . ." David M. Raup and J. John Sepkoski, Jr., "Periodicity of Extinctions in the Geologic Past," *Proc. Natl. Acad. Sci. USA,* vol. 81, pp. 801–5, (February 1984), p. 805.

"I got a crazy paper from Raup and Sepkoski . . ." Richard Muller, *Nemesis: The Death Star* (New York: Weidenfeld & Nicolson), 1988, p. 3.

"Suppose we found a way to make an asteroid hit the earth every 26 million years . . ." Richard Muller, *Nemesis: The Death Star* (New York: Weidenfeld & Nicolson), 1988, p. 7ff.

Page 164

". . . 'dark matter' might take the form of *brown* dwarfs . . ." Brown dwarfs are out of fashion in astronomical circles at this writing, owing to studies that seem to rule out their presence in binary star systems, to which the majority of known stars belong. But in my opinion, we still know too little about how stars form to abandon the hypothesis that there may indeed be lots of small, dim ones around.

Page 165

"Impact theory is still the subject of active controversy . . ." For a review of the extinction debate see Stephen K. Donovan, ed., *Mass Extinctions: Processes and Evidence* (New York: Columbia University Press, 1989).

"The prospect of a celestial mechanism . . ." Comets may also have influenced terrestrial affairs without having struck the earth, simply by hanging around. In one recent paper, two scientists propose that amino acids found above and below the KT layer could have come from comet dust spewed into the inner solar system by a giant comet trapped in an orbit near Earth's. See David Grinspoon and Kevin Zahnle, "Comet Dust as a Source of Amino Acids at the Cretaceous-Tertiary Boundary," *Nature*, vol. 348 (November 8, 1990), pp. 157ff.

Page 166

". . . a small marine fish from the Gulf of California . . ." The saga of *bairdiella* in the Salton Sea is discussed in Steven M. Stanley, *The New Evolutionary Timetable* (New York: Basic Books, 1981), pp. 120–21.

Page 168

"Had it not been for the large comet . . ." Richard A. Muller, "An Adventure in Science," *The New York Times Magazine*, March 24, 1985, p. 50.

THE MANICHEAN HERESY

Page 171

"Dear Posterity . . ." In Helen Dukas and Banesh Hoffman, eds., *Albert Einstein, The Human Side: New Glimpses From His Archives* (Princeton University Press, 1979), p. 105.

"Some races wax and others wane . . ." Lucretius, *De Rerum Natura*, trans. Cyril Bailey (Oxford University Press, 1947, 1972), p. 241.

Page 175

"See my charred hair." Ovid, *Metamorphoses*, Book II, trans. Horace Gregory (New York: Viking, 1958), pp. 39–40.

Page 176

"We have the power to inaugurate events totally beyond our control." Kosta Tsipis, *Arsenal: Understanding Weapons in the Nuclear Age* (New York: Simon & Schuster, 1983), p. 101.

Page 177

"Then Phaëthon / Numbed, chilled, and broken, dropped the reins." Ovid, *Metamorphoses*, Book II, trans. Horace Gregory (New York: Viking, 1958), pp. 36–37.

Page 178

"Evolution has made countless mistakes . . ." In Arne Tiselius and Sam Nilsson, eds., *The Place of Value in a World of Fact* (New York: Wiley, 1970), p. 298.

Page 180

"I don't know how many future generations we can count on before the Lord returns." In Charles Krauthammer, "The End of the World," *The New Republic* (March 28, 1983), p. 12.

"Not a matter of opinion, but scientific certainty . . ." Charles Krauthammer, "The End of the World," *The New Republic* (March 28, 1983), p. 12.

". . . the biologist Paul Ehrlich predicted . . ." See Paul Ehrlich, *The Population Bomb* (New York: Ballantine, 1968).

Page 181

"It is very difficult to make an accurate prediction . . ." In M. Taub, *Evolution of Matter and Energy,* unnumbered manuscript page, 1986.

Page 183

"The Manichean heresy . . ." In David Castronovo, *Edmund Wilson* (New York: Ungar, 1984), p. 61.

Page 184

". . . we have at least an hypothesis which can be followed up . . ." In Timothy Ferris, *The Red Limit* (New York: Morrow, 1983), p. 46.

Page 185

"Wait and see!" In Helen Dukas and Banesh Hoffman, eds., *Albert Einstein, The Human Side: New Glimpses From His Archives* (Princeton University Press, 1979), p. 34.

THE LIBRARY OF THE AMAZON

Page 187

"In the vast Library . . ." Jorge Luis Borges, "The Library of Babel," in his *Labyrinths* (New York: New Directions, 1964), p. 54.

"Hell is truth seen too late." In Norman Myers ed., *Gaia: An Atlas of Planet Management* (New York: Anchor/Doubleday, 1984), p. 159.

". . . a tenth of the Amazon is gone." The situation in Brazil has improved somewhat since 1988. President Fernando Collor de Mello has signed a decree banning all cutting and exploitation of native vegetation in Brazil's decimated Atlantic Forest, while legislative and law-enforcement improvements resulted, in 1990, in a twenty-five percent reduction in the amount of Amazon jungle cleared annually for ranching.

Page 188

"A pond in Brazil . . ." These examples of biological diversity in rain forests are drawn principally from studies by Terry Erwin of the Smithsonian Institution, and Peter Ashton and Edward O. Wilson of Harvard University.

Page 189

". . . the folly that our descendants are least likely to forgive us." In Norman Myers, ed., *Gaia: An Atlas of Planet Management* (New York: Anchor/Doubleday, 1984), p. 159.

Page 192

". . . computers use *algorithms*." The word *algorithm* is a corruption of Al Kworesmi, the name of a ninth-century Arab mathematician whose book on the subject was influential in Renaissance Europe.

Page 195

"Too great even to conceive, let alone duplicate." Edward O. Wilson, "Threats to Biodiversity," *Scientific American* (September 1989), p. 114.

Page 196

"American consumers spent twelve billion dollars on pharmaceuticals." N. R. Farnsworth and D. D Soejarto, "Potential Consequences of Plant Extinction in the United States on the Current and Future Availability of Prescription Drugs," *Economic Botany* 39 (3) (1985), pp. 231–40.

Pages 196–97

"A single shaman of the Wayana tribe . . ." Mark J. Plotkin, "The Healing Forest: The Search for New Jungle Medicines," *The Futurist* (January 1990), p. 9.

Page 197

"The Indians are disappearing." It is estimated that six to twelve million Indians populated the Amazon when Columbus reached America, and that only two hundred thousand are alive today. See Susanna Hecht and Alexander Cockburn, *The Fate of the Forest: Developers, Destroyers and Defenders of the Amazon* (New York: Harper, 1990), p. 3.

"Of all the shamans with whom I have lived . . ." Mark J. Plotkin, "The Healing Forest: The Search for New Jungle Medicines," *The Futurist* (January 1990), p. 9.

Page 199

"A new salient of knowledge is being created . . ." Heinz Pagels, *The Dreams of Reason: The Computer and the Rise of the Sciences of Complexity* (New York: Simon & Schuster, 1988), p. 150.

IT

Page 201

"The world is the totality of facts, not of things." Ludwig Wittgenstein, *Tractatus Logico-Philosophicus,* trans. C.K. Ogden (London: Routledge, 1988), 1.1.

"The subject matter of research is no longer nature in itself . . ." In Aldous Huxley, *Literature and Science* (New York: Harper & Row, 1963), p. 76.

"Mind and universe." In an important sense the mind is a creation of the universe and the universe is a creation of the mind. I don't mean that the universe doesn't exist, but merely that the concept of a "universe"—and all we can ever know about it—must necessarily reside in the mind. This I take to be the position of the more undogmatic among those philosophers who assert that "it's all in the mind." Its spirit was exemplified in a 1990 conversation between Tenzin Gyatso, the fourteenth Dalai Lama, and my friend Alex Shoumatoff. Inquiring about the Buddhist belief that objects are but a projection of mental images, Shoumatoff told the Dalai Lama that the night before he'd awakened in his hotel room and tripped over his suitcase in the dark while searching for the light switch. "You can't tell me the suitcase was just in my mind," Shoumatoff said. "I didn't even know it was there until I tripped on it." The Dalai Lama chuckled. "But what is a suitcase?" he asked. "You can describe the color, shape, size, weight, and material of the suitcase, but still there is something else. At the quantum mechanical level there *is* no suitcase, and if you were a subatomic particle you could pass right through the suitcase. If you analyze it, you can find the independent existence of neither the suitcase nor yourself. But that does not mean that they do not exist at all."

Page 201

". . . actively searching for things to see . . ." J. Z. Young, *Programs of the Brain* (New York: Oxford University Press, 1978), p. 117.

Page 204

"Uncertainty principle." As often happens with scientific discoveries, the language used to describe Heisenberg's finding tends to obscure its significance; "uncertainty" implies a temporary limitation of one's knowledge, whereas the whole point of Heisenberg's principle is that we can *never* extract all the information about a subatomic system. The physicist and historian of science Abraham Pais writes that "it might have been better had the term 'unknowability relation' been used." The physicist Victor Weisskopf opts for "limiting relation." My own preference is "indeterminacy principle." But, as Pais points out, "One neither can nor should do anything about that now." See Abraham Pais, *Inward Bound* (New York: Oxford University Press, 1986), p. 262, and Victor Weisskopf, *The Joy of Insight: Passions of a Physicist* (New York: Basic Books, 1991), Chapter 3.

Page 205

"Whereof one cannot speak, thereof one must be silent." Ludwig Wittgenstein, *Tractatus Logico-Philosophicus*, trans. C.K. Ogden (London: Routledge, 1988), p. 189.

"The famous 'dual slit' experiment . . ." For a more detailed discussion of the dual slit experiment, see Richard P. Feynman, Robert B. Leighton, and Matthew Sands, *The Feynman Lectures of Physics* (Reading, Mass.: Addison-Wesley, 1963), vol. III, chapter 1.

Page 208

"If anybody says he can think about quantum problems without getting giddy, that only shows he has not understand the first thing about them." In Ruth Moore, *Niels Bohr* (Cambridge, Mass.: MIT Press, 1985), p. 127.

Page 210

"Entropy." The concept of entropy arose from the research of some of the nineteenth century's greatest scientists, notably Sadi Carnot, James Joule, Lord Kelvin, Rudolf Clausius, and, especially, Ludwig Boltzmann. For a review see P.W. Atkins, *The Second Law* (New York: Freeman, 1984).

Page 213

"Bits." The term *bit*, I am advised, was coined by John Tukey, later of Princeton University, in a September 1, 1947, Bell Laboratories memorandum titled "Sequential Conversion of Continuous Data to Digital Data."

Page 215

". . . human creativity seems to reduce the amount of entropy . . ." See Leon Brillouin, *Scientific Uncertainty, and Information* (New York: Academic Press, 1964), p. 21.

Page 216

". . . the brain is a 'Turing machine' . . ." For an analysis see Donald H. Perkel, "Logical Neurons: The Enigmatic Legacy of Warren McCulough," *Trends in Neurosciences* (January 1988), p. 10; also George Johnson, *In the Palaces of Memory* (New York: Knopf, 1991), p. 127.

Page 217

"Biological reproduction can be likened to a communications channel . . ." For an analysis of how biological replication may be viewed this way, see Lila L. Gatlin, *Information Theory and the Living System* (New York: Columbia University Press, 1972).

Page 218

"Quantum." John Wheeler notes that "quantum" is German for "hunk." Under wartime rationing, each German received his *quantum* of bread and margarine. Wheeler writes that "one can only adequately convey in English the flavor of Planck's 'quantum theory' by calling it the 'hunk theory' of radiation."

"It from bit . . ." John Archibald Wheeler, "Information, Physics, Quantum: The Search for Links," *Proc. 3rd Int Symp. Foundations of Quantum Mechanics,* Tokyo, 1989, p. 355.

"No phenomenon *is* a phenomenon until it is an *observed* phenomenon." John Archibald Wheeler, "Delayed-Choice Experiments and the Bohr-Einstein Dialogue," London, American Philosophical Society and the Royal Society, papers read at a meeting, June 5, 1980, p. 25. For a technical discussion of the question of observation in quantum mechanics, see John Archibald Wheeler and Wojciech Hubert Zurek, eds., *Quantum Theory and Measurement* (Princeton, N.J.: Princeton University Press, 1983).

Page 220

"An observer participates in the making of meaning." John Archibald Wheeler, "Information, Physics, Quantum: The Search for Links," *Proc. 3rd Int. Symp. Foundations of Quantum Mechanics,* Tokyo, 1989, p. 360.

Page 221

"How far foot and ferry have carried meaning-making communication . . ." John Archibald Wheeler, "Information, Physics, Quantum: The Search for Links," *Proc. 3rd Int. Symp. Foundations of Quantum Mechanics,* Tokyo, 1989, p. 360.

Index

A

African-Americans, 127
Africans, 127
Afterlife, 139
  and NDEs, 137–38
Aggressiveness scenario, 181–83
Agora (Athens), 51
AIDS, drugs useful in treating, 196
Air and the Song, The (Magritte), 4
Akutagawa, Ryunosuke, 205
Alchemists, 9–10
Algorithms, 192–93
al-Hārith, 60
Aliens, 40, 66. *See also* Extraterrestrials.
Alonso (fictional character), 44
Alvarez, Luis, 154, 162–63
Alvarez, Walter, 152–54, 156, 157
Alvarezes, the, 155, 159
Alyosha (fictional character), 28
Amazon forests, destruction of, 187–88, 190, 196–200
America. *See* United States.
Ames Research Center (NASA), 21, 49

Amino acids, 23, 217
Amos and Andy (fictional characters), 133
Amplification, process of, 219, 221
AM radio, data-handling capacity of, 47
Anaxagoras, 19
Anderson, Flipper, 101–2
Andromeda galaxy, 42
Animal Mother (fictional character), 99
Antarctic ice cap, 159
Apollo (god), 175, 177
Apollo program, 120–21, 122, 125
Aquinas, Thomas, 89
Archimedes, 111
Arctic peoples, 127
Aristotle, 19, 95, 197
Artificial reality. *See* Virtual reality.
Asaro, Frank, 154
Astaire, Fred, 104
Asteroids, 154, 155, 159, 162–63
Athletes, 100–15
"Auguries of Innocence" (Blake), 92
"Authoritativeness," in Zen, 88